NEW BARS & RESTAURANTS 2

NEW BARS & RESTAURANTS 2

Daniela Santos Quartino

NEW BARS & RESTAURANTS 2

For information, address Collins Design,
10 East 53rd Street, New York, NY 10022.

HarperCollins books may be purchased for
educational, business, or sales promotional use.
For information, please write: Special Markets
Department, HarperCollins*Publishers*,
10 East 53rd Street, New York, NY 10022.

First published in 2010 by:
Collins Design
An Imprint of HarperCollins*Publishers*
10 East 53rd Street
New York, NY 10022
Tel.: (212) 207-7000
Fax: (212) 207-7654
collinsdesign@harpercollins.com
www.harpercollins.com

Distributed throughout the world by:
HarperCollins*Publishers*
10 East 53rd Street
New York, NY 10022
Fax: (212) 207-7654

Editorial Coordinator:
Simone K. Schleifer

Assistant to Editorial Coordinator:
Aitana Lleonart

Editor and Text Writer:
Daniela Santos Quartino

Art Director:
Mireia Casanovas Soley

Design and Layout Coordinator:
Claudia Martínez Alonso

Cover Layout:
María Eugenia Castell Carballo

Layout:
Yolanda G. Román

ISBN: 978-0-06-196881-5
Library of Congress Control Number: 2010927840

Printed in Spain
First Printing, 2010

Contents

Introduction

Decor is one of the three pillars that determine the success of a restaurant, along with the quality of the food and customer service. Cheaper travel and globalization, which has led to the expansion of chains, offers greater access to high-quality fare, and consequently, diners have become more demanding.

Media has also contributed to our expanding knowledge of cuisine, leading to more television programs and publications dedicated to gastronomy and to the birth of a new generation of chefs, who are rated by Michelin stars or by audience ratings. Not surprisingly, open-plan kitchens, characteristic of Asian culture, where diners can watch chefs at work, have become one of the latest trends in restaurants worldwide.

Sectorization, the creation of different ambiences within one space, has also become a popular new trend in the architecture and interior design of restaurants and bars. Private booths and tables with differences in height, intimate lounges, different styles of furniture, and even diverse lighting have remade overcrowded establishments and now provide multiple dining environments within a single restaurant or bar.

Today, restaurants appeal to all senses and seek to establish an emotional bond with diners who are eager to discover a range of experiences that go beyond the limitations of a dish. The gorgeous establishments included here were chosen for their aesthetic value and creative ambiances.

Americas

Pio Pio Restaurant

This restaurant, specializing in Peruvian cuisine and located in Hell's Kitchen, New York City, is disbursed onto three floors. The ground-level houses the lobby, the lounge, the main bar, and places to sit down. The main dining area is located downstairs in an area that is twice the height of the lobby, and in close proximity to the kitchen.

The form of the area is defined by four boxes that were constructed like installations within a frame. Three of these boxes have wooden cladding. The fourth is covered with ocotillo poles. The first and smallest of these is located near the entrance, which is where the patrons are welcomed to the establishment. The restaurant services and the lounge are contained in the second, which is larger in size. The third one houses several booths. The main dining area, the fourth one contained inside an ocotillo box, is decorated with mural-sized photos of the Andes.

Designer: SEBASTIAN MARISCAL STUDIO
www.piopionyc.com
Location: NEW YORK, NY, USA
Opening date: AUGUST 2009
Photos: © PAÚL RIVERA

AS SOON AS THE PATRONS STEP INSIDE, THEY ARE CONFRONTED WITH INTERIOR VIEWS THAT ARE CONTROLLED AND RESTRICTED TO MAINTAIN THE FOCUS OF ATTENTION ON EACH OF THE MANY INTERCONNECTING SPACES INSIDE THIS RESTAURANT.

Cement structures contrast with the natural warmth of the ocotillo cladding.

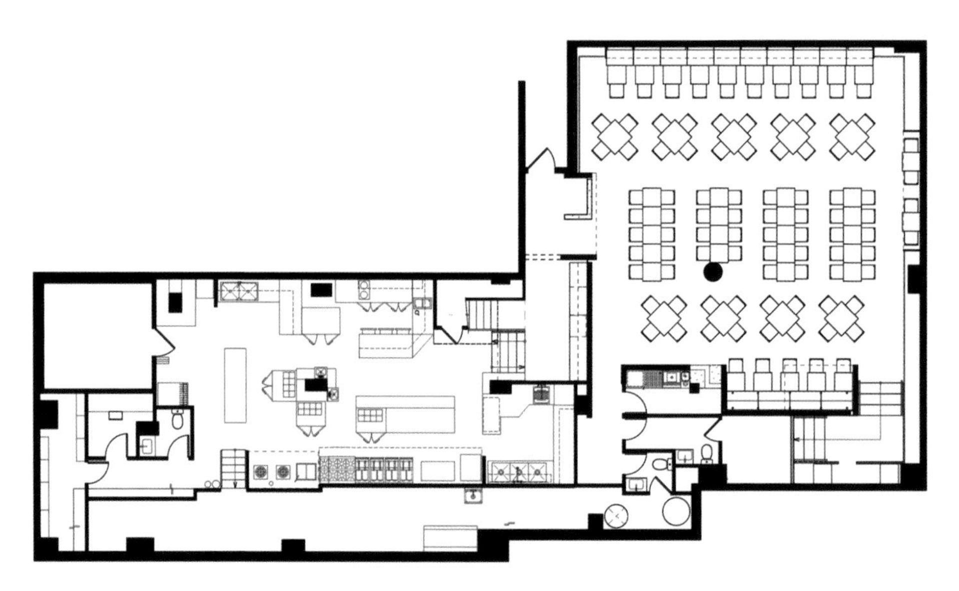

Floor plan

Urban Farmer

This modern brasserie situated in the central lobby of a luxury hotel incorporates wooden decks and semi-enclosed spaces into its design. The country-chic style achieved by its architects is complemented by the use of a variety of natural materials, such as wood, leather, and stone.

The restaurant has a large deck that seems to be outdoors, not only because of the abundant natural light entering the lobby, but also because of the presence of green in the form of wheatgrass plants. Its "pantry" is a more intimate space, featuring steel and wooden walls lined with shelves that hold cans of colorful fruits and vegetables in glass jars. The "library," adjacent to the hotel lobby, is a quieter space, containing three hundred books, a pool table, and twenty-four pieces of original art from local artists.

Designer: D-ASH DESIGN
www.urbanfarmerrestaurant.com
Location: PORTLAND, OR, USA
Opening date: DECEMBER 2008
Photos: © MICHAEL MATHERS

THIS MODERN, CHIC COUNTRY-STYLE BRASSERIE IS LOCATED IN THE LOBBY OF THE HOTEL. ITS ABUNDANT NATURAL LIGHT AND GREEN PLANTS GIVE THE IMPRESSION OF AN OUTDOOR SPACE.

The bar is a twenty-three feet (seven meters) long piece of pine wood, which originally was part of a houseboat.

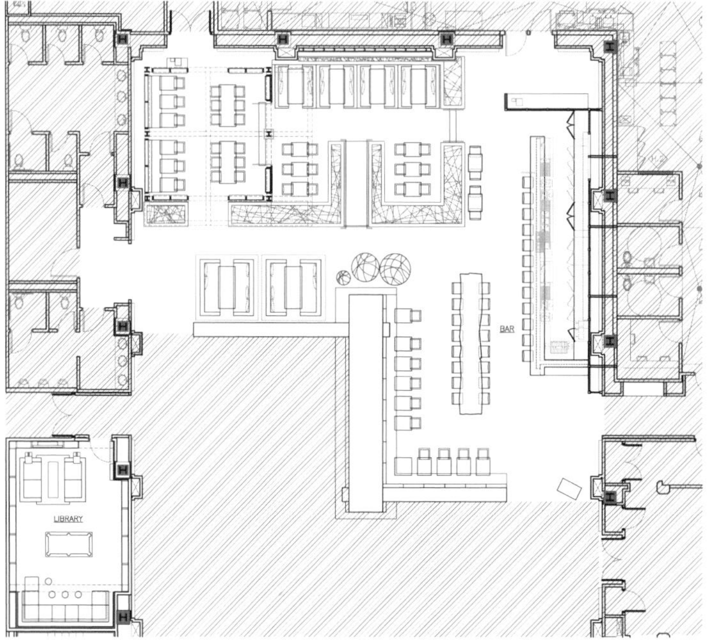

Floor plan

COCKER SPANIELS
Henri Rochefort
THE SACRED PATH
GONE ARE THE DAYS
cock

Park Avenue

Not only do the ingredients at this restaurant change with the seasons, but so does the space itself. Individual palettes of color, as well as menu modifications, are implemented at the start of each season: summer, fall, winter, and spring.

The voyages of Captain James Cook, a British explorer, served as inspiration for the restaurant core interior design elements and its corporate graphics. Taking the "sandwich islands" as a starting point for the eye, the artwork featured around the restaurant in the summer has prints with fish in white and yellow. Fall art pays homage to sailing and borrows the copper and ocher tones prevalent in the constellations. Winter art alludes to the voyages made by Cook to the Antarctic Circle, and uses white as a prevailing color. Spring art takes its inspiration from Cook's voyage to New Zealand and uses a variety of purples and golds.

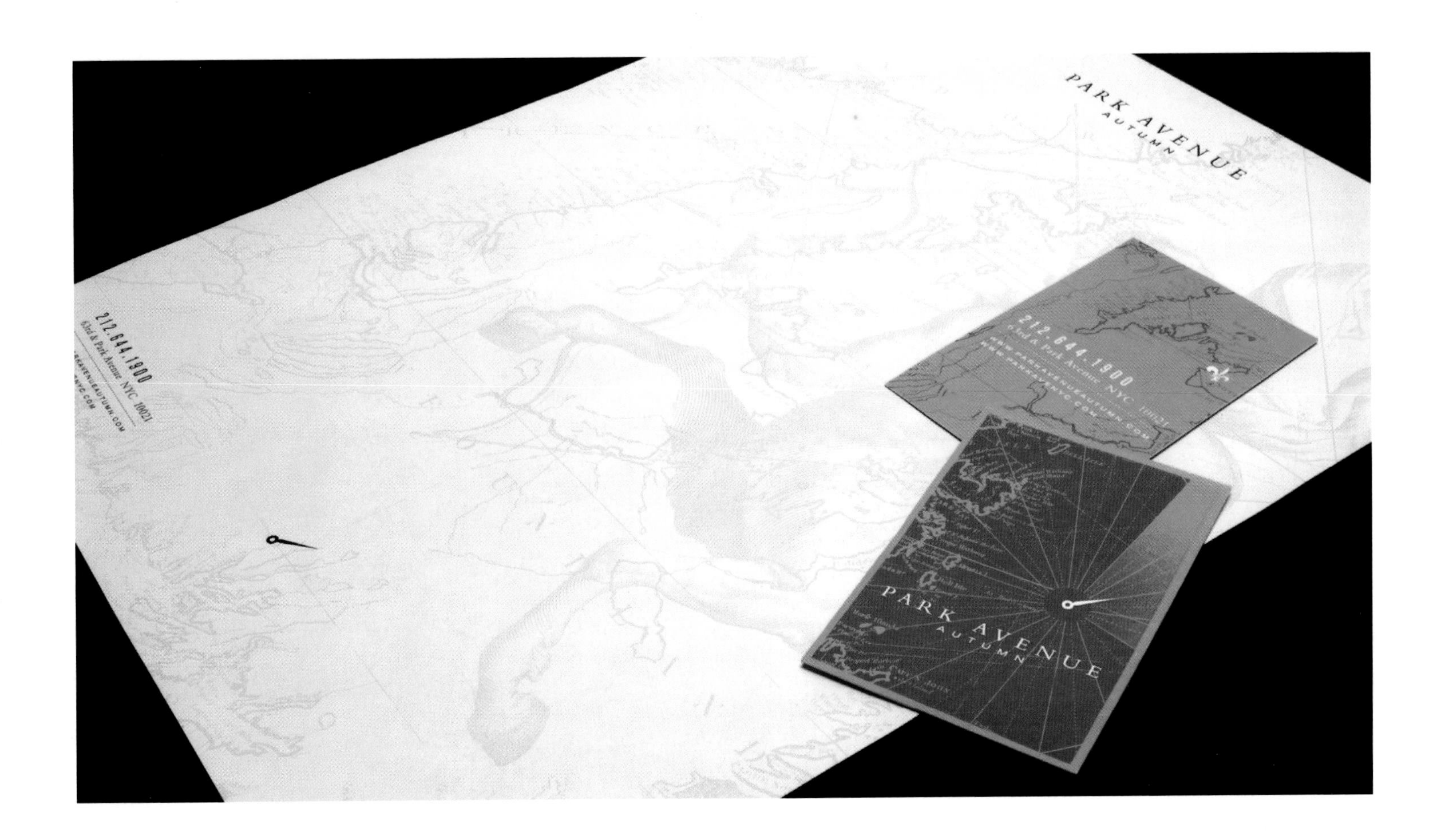

Designer: AVROKO
www.parkavenyc.com
Location: NEW YORK, NY, USA
Opening date: JUNE 2007
Photos: © MICHAEL WEBER

AT THE BEGINNING OF EACH SEASON, THE RESTAURANT CLOSES FOR TWO DAYS AND REINVENTS ITSELF. IT THEN REOPENS WITH A NEW NAME, MENU, AND DÉCOR.

Reversible cushions, removable panels on the walls and ceiling, and various types of tablecloths all contribute to the change in the restaurant's appearance each season.

KNOB
CREEK

an with
u see behi
e lived a
ed and co
stand a
t the cro
e left you
sterday
your ye
s behind
to tomo
charro y
yesterday
ayed a m
pray for
you left

Charro Restaurante

Using a "Latin fusion" label, this restaurant presents traditional Mexican food in the form of a new culinary experience. Its interior décor is chock-full of references to the Elvis Presley film *Charro!*

A large part of the restaurant's surfaces are covered with lyrics of songs from the film scribbled in white. In some cases, they emerge through crosses cut out of the red paneling. A stronger red than that used on the paneling is used in the bar's most striking feature, its acrylic mosaics.

A variation in the restaurant's theme, but following the same style, is found in a private room inside the dining area, where gothic-style lighting of the type found in Mexican churches contrasts with the decorative wallpaper. The restaurant also contains a second bar area downstairs, as well as a large area reserved for private parties. Although decorated in different tones and created with different materials, these areas have the same stylistic identity as the main dining room.

Designer: SLICK+DESIGN
www.charrorestaurante.com
Location: MILWAUKEE, WI, USA
Opening date: DECEMBER 2008
Photos: © NICOLE D. ZENONI

FROM ITS NAME TO THE MOST SIGNIFICANT ASPECTS OF ITS INTERIOR DESIGN, THIS RESTAURANT IS STEEPED IN REFERENCES TO THE FILM *CHARRO!*, STARRING ELVIS PRESLEY.

The chairs with black or white vinyl upholstery contrast with the rustic style of the tables they surround, which were made in a style reminiscent of medieval times.

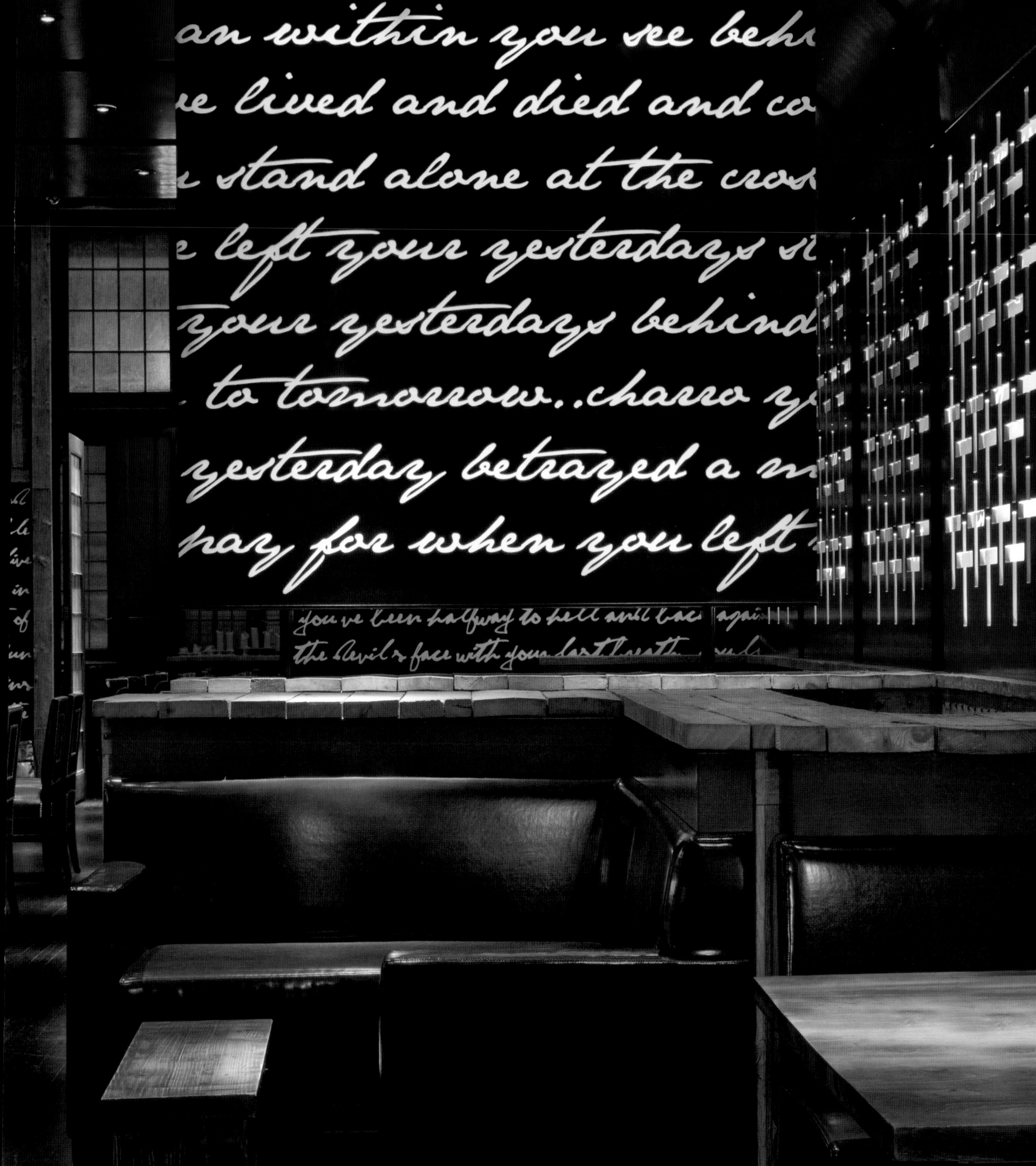

an within you see beh
e lived and died and co
stand alone at the cros
e left your yesterdays si
your yesterdays behind
to tomorrow..charro y
yesterday betrayed a m
pay for when you left

who makes me always tremble with
who makes my temperature rise! who makes
who makes my heart beat like thunder!
wonderful rapture with one burning glance, from her
tame then suddenly i saw marguerita and i was
lips have made me her prisoner a slave to her
of her hand marguerita...sweet...

The Wright

In celebration of the fiftieth anniversary of the Guggenheim Museum, which was designed by Frank Lloyd Wright, this 1,600 square foot (148 square meters) restaurant opened to the public in 2009. Its dynamic lines and preponderance of white reflect the design of the rest of the legendary building located in New York's Upper East Side.

Distinguishing features of the restaurant's design include a curvilinear walnut wall layered with illuminated fiber-optics, a bar clad in white Corian, vivid blue leather seats, and a layered ceiling canopy of taut white membrane that evokes the forms of the building.

The restaurant seats fifty-eight people at individual tables, and other larger tables with booths covered in white fabric. Once comfortably seated, diners can taste the organic and sustainable cuisine prepared by Rodolfo Contreras, a Mexican chef recommended to the restaurant by chef David Bouley.

Designer: ANDRE KIKOSKI ARCHITECT
www.guggenheim.org
Location: NEW YORK, NY, USA
Opening date: DECEMBER 2009
Photos: © PETER AARON

"WE CHOSE A PALETTE OF MATERIALS AND COLORS THAT STAND TO GIVE THE SPACE DYNAMIC, SOBER, AND ELEGANT FORMS," SAID ANDRE KIKOSKI, A LEAD ARCHITECT BEHIND THE RESTAURANT'S DESIGN.

A colorful sculpture by British artist Liam Gillick consists of several aluminum sheets mounted on the walls and ceiling.

Brand Steakhouse

Located on the same floor as the casino in the Monte Carlo Resort, the center of attention in this restaurant is the ceiling, with 255 aluminum panels clad in leather. Positioned side-by-side, their prints create an abstract, pixelized image, a look reinforced by bright lighting, which accentuates the spaces between the panels. The prints were transferred from digital files to a synthetic material, which was then stuck onto the panels.

The main dining room, lounge, and private area of the restaurant have their own looks, but are not unrelated. The main dining room has three areas marked off by split-level flooring. Its focal point is a large graphic that simulates a number of shiny tree branches above a bronze mirror. A variety of sliding glass doors and bronze curtains provide a somewhat ambiguous partition with enticing glimpses of the casino, offering guests the opportunity to engage in social contact and observation of the action from afar.

Designer: GRAFT
www.lightgroup.com
Location: LAS VEGAS, NV, USA
Opening date: SUMMER 2009
Photos: © RICARDO RIDECOS

LIMIT SLOTS
PLAYERS CLUB

THE COMBINATION OF TEXTURES AND SHAPES WITH THE VARYING HEIGHTS AND SIZES OF THE 255 PANELS ON THE CEILING EVOKE A SPATIAL EXPERIENCE THAT IS CONSTANTLY SHIFTING.

The oak on the floor, the leather on the panels, the suede upholstery, the bronze, and the animal print generate a feeling of nature and wildlife, which contrasts with the highly synthetic atmosphere of the casino.

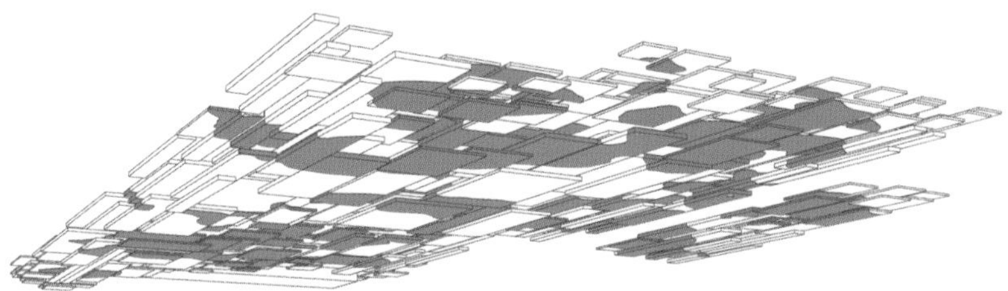

Axonometry

Beijing Noodle No. 9

Located in Las Vegas' Caesars Palace Hotel and Resort, the design of this Chinese restaurant took advantage of the lack of supporting columns in the building to offer an open-plan layout. The aim was to use the repetition of a graphic motif to create a minimalist atmosphere.

Because the restaurant is located next to the casino, the dividing line between the two was purposefully blurred by means of an open facade, which dulls the sounds coming from the gaming room, but allows diners to continue to watch the excitement. As the visitors walk further into the restaurant, they are immersed in a surrealist atmosphere created by decorated surfaces. Arabesques, spread around the steel sheeting on the walls, gradually merge with the ceiling and generate an interior reminiscent of a bud.

The cohesion in the restaurant's design is enhanced by the use of LED lights positioned between the different layers of the bud. The lights cause the shadows of the arabesques to be projected onto the tables, floor, and kitchen area.

Designer: YUHKICHI KAWAI/DESIGN SPIRITS
www.caesarspalace.com
Location: LAS VEGAS, NV, USA
Opening date: JANUARY 2009
Photos: © BARRY JOHNSON

THE FISH IN THE TANKS ARE ALL OF THE SAME COLOR, WHICH MATCHES WITH THE GLASSES AND THE JARS CONTAINING COOKING INGREDIENTS.

The arabesques are repeated on all surfaces. The bright light and feeling of lightness and air envelop the diners in a sensual and visually relaxing ambience.

EXIT

The Chefs' House Restaurant

Forming part of the prestigious George Brown College Chef School, this restaurant is located in a refurbished industrial building. In keeping with the latest trends in the culinary world, huge street-side windows allow a perfect view into its kitchen. A colored glass foyer contrasts with the rustic finish of the walls' bare brickwork. The industrial-style kitchen is equipped with stainless steel throughout, which contrasts with its bright red tile and glass counter.

The dining area has a more intimate look than the kitchen, thanks to the corrugated panels that cover part of the original wooden ceiling and which absorb excess noise, and the well-placed fluorescent lighting. The lights are low-watt bulbs arranged in a way so that from outside, they have the appearance of sparks floating in space.

Designer: KEARNS MANCINI ARCHITECTS;
GOW HASTINGS ARCHITECTS
www.thechefshouse.com
Location: TORONTO, CANADA
Opening date: SPRING 2009
Photos: © TOM ARBAN PHOTOGRAPHY

THE DESIGN OF THIS SPACE ENABLES BOTH DINERS AND PASSERSBY TO WITNESS THE LIVE SHOW PUT ON BY THE CHEFS AS THEY GO ABOUT THEIR WORK.

The worktops line the windows in such a way that the chefs take on the appearance of live mannequins bestowing their own idiosyncrasies on the restaurant.

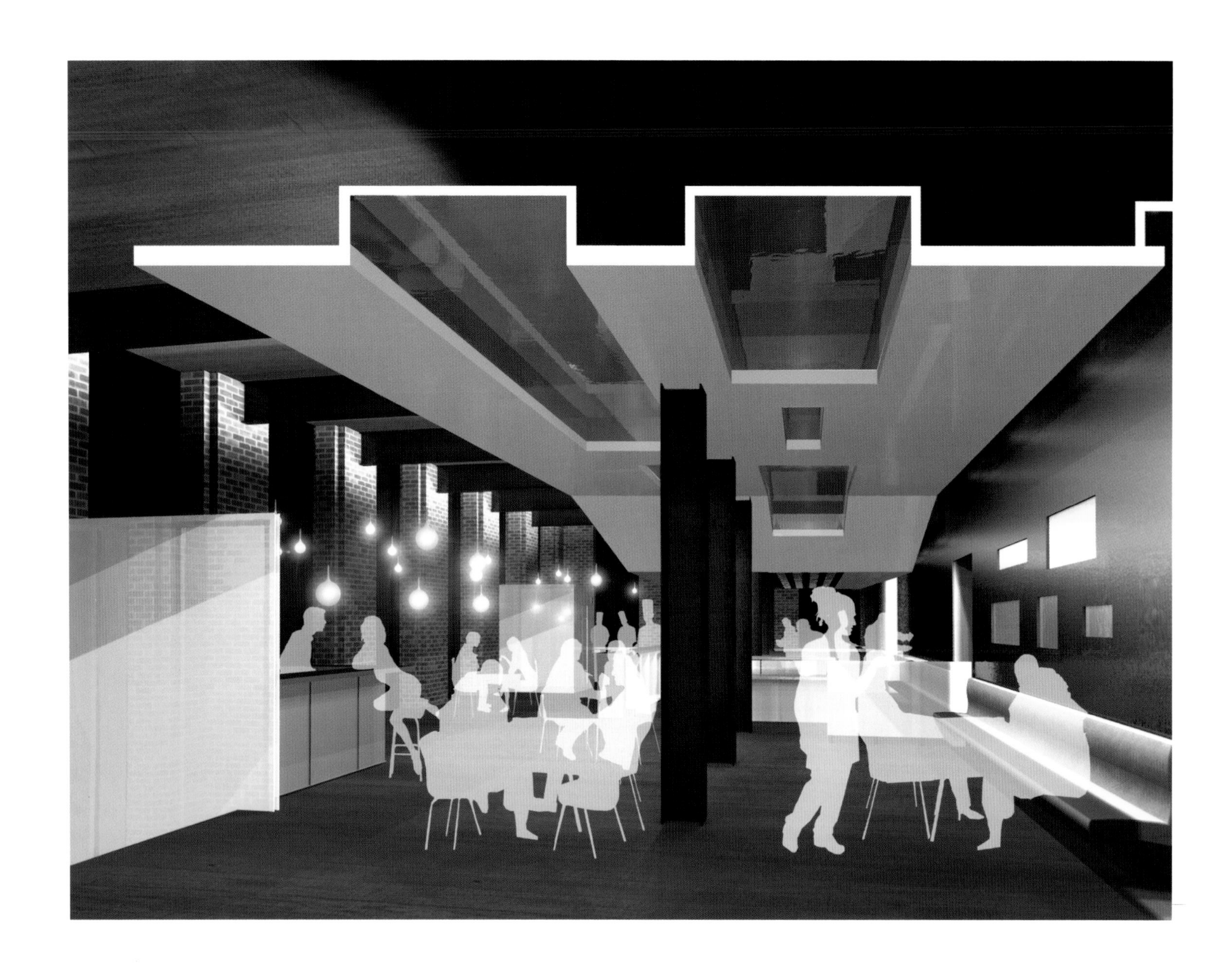

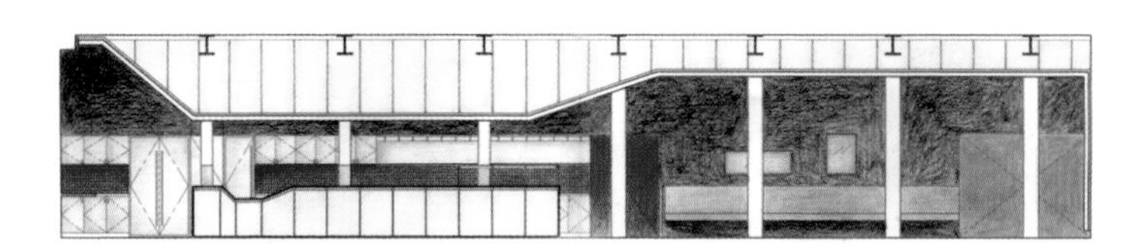

Section

Floor plan

The Standard Grill and The Standard Club

In contrast with the Brutalist style of the Standard Hotel building, which soars eighteen floors above High Lane and was designed in harmony with the historical context of the area, its new restaurant is more colorful and reliant on natural elements.

The venue has a terrace, an indoor bar with a cafeteria, and a private area. While there is a predominance of light colors, porcelain, and steel in the bar, the restaurant was mainly decorated with wood, bronze, and copper tones. The designers drew inspiration from Brazilian design, which emphasizes natural woods and organic forms. The effect is a style reminiscent of the clubs of the 1940s—with special attention given to luxurious materials.

The height of the hotel meant that it was possible to design what appears to be a huge tree rising from behind the bar, up the wall, and spreading its branches throughout the club. The ceiling, clad in gold discs, works as a mirror reflecting the activity that takes place in the club.

Designer: ROMAN & WILLIAMS
www.thestandardgrill.com
Location: NEW YORK, NY, USA
Opening date: JUNE AND SEPTEMBER 2009
Photos: © STEPHEN ALESCH

THE RESTAURANT AND BAR-CLUB AT THE STANDARD HOTEL DRAW INSPIRATION FROM THE SENSUAL EXUBERANCE OF ITS NATURAL ELEMENTS, IN CONTRAST WITH THE BRUTALIST STYLE OF THE BUILDING, WHICH IS ROOTED IN THE HISTORICAL CONTEXT OF THE LOCAL AREA.

The bar-club and restaurant have contrasting colors and materials, but maintain a common style based on the historical context of the Meatpacking District.

EXIT

Delicatessen

Delicatessen is part of a typical early-twentieth-century brick building in SoHo, New York City, where modern and classical architecture exist side by side. The large openings, in both the front and the glass courtyard, give the urban environment an important visual prominence in the restaurant.

The dining room features items such as stainless steel and glass garage doors, which take up the entire façade, leaving the establishment wide open when they are pulled up toward the ceiling. The walls are made of wood planks from old barns in Vermont and contrast with the front of the bar, which is equipped with a glass shelf lined with colorful drawings and paintings.

The basement is accessed via a spacious wooden staircase. This space is home to a minibar and the Courtyard lounge, beneath a glass atrium dominated by a large mural by local artist Juan José Heredia.

Designer: NEMA WORKSHOP
www.delicatessennyc.com
Location: NEW YORK, NY, USA
Opening date: JULY 2008
Photos: © DAVID JOSEPH

THE SPIRIT OF NEW YORK'S SOHO SLIPS INTO THE INTERIOR OF THIS RESTAURANT AND BAR THROUGH A FACADE THAT OPENS FULLY AND A SPECTACULAR GLASS ATRIUM INSIDE.

The long horizontal mirrors are repeated both in the main dining room, on the first floor, and in the basement's glass-roof patio.

Toast

From the moment you enter this restaurant, you have the sensation of strolling around inside a large loaf of sliced bread. This effect is due to the wooden panelling on all its surfaces, which is randomly perforated with holes of various shapes and sizes.

A large horizontal plate suspended in midair extends from the entrance to the main part of the building over the bar. At one end, the plate gives way to a hollow hanging column with cavities for the storage of bottles and glasses. The bar area uses a similar design at ground level, matching the shape of the cupola and extending beneath it.

The dining area includes large communal tables, as well as smaller tables to seat fewer people, and booths. The open kitchen has a bar with bar stools for patrons to watch the chefs and pizza makers at work. A fireplace with shelving for storage purposes provides warmth.

Designer: STANLEY SAITOWITZ/NATOMA ARCHITECTS INC.
www.toastnovato.com
Location: NOVATO, CA, USA
Opening date: SUMMER 2009
Photos: © RIEN VAN RIJTHOVEN

THE PERFORATIONS AND COLOR OF THE PANELING IS REMINISCENT OF SLICES OF BREAD, HENCE THE NAME OF THE RESTAURANT.

The wall to the left of the entrance has a generous amount of shelving for the storage of ingredients and utensils.

CASA SOLANA
PINTO BEANS
Arezzio
Mr Espresso

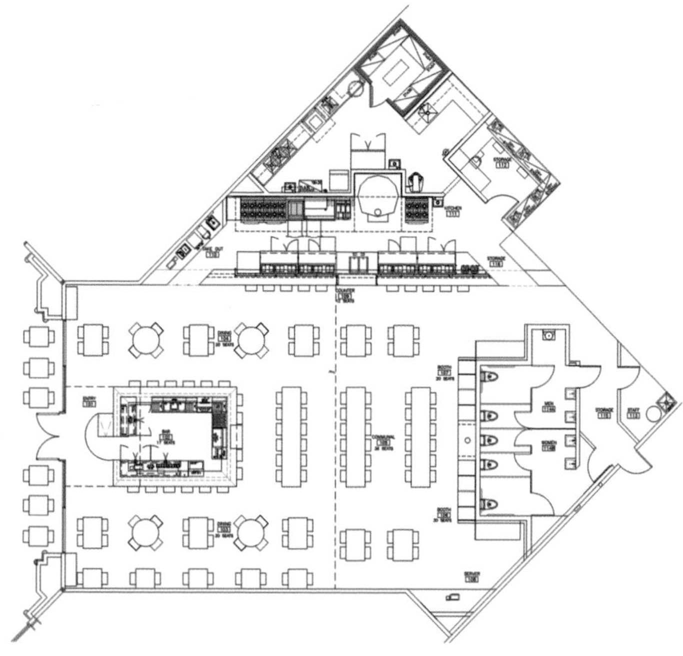

Floor plan

The Bazaar by José Andrés

This restaurant, a part of the SLS Beverly Hills Hotel, exemplifies luxury, sophistication, and provocation, like the rest of the hotel. Its large open space is divided into different sections, each distinguished by its own specific palette of colors and style of furniture. For example, La Patisserie, one of the sections, is characterized by hues of pink and silver and has a light-hearted Victorian vibe to it, which contrasts with the sober and formal Bar Centro section.

Spanish chef José Andrés, who is famous in America thanks to his TV show *Made in Spain*, is in charge of the menu. While inspired by traditional Iberian cuisine, Andrés has given the menu a modern touch; offering up liquid nitrogen caipirinha filled cones or foie gras wrapped in cotton candy, and whetting the appetites of visitors from around the world.

Designer: PHILIPPE STARCK
www.thebazaar.com
Location: LOS ANGELES, CA, USA
Opening date: SUMMER 2008
Photos: © JAMES MERRELL

DESIGNED BY PHILIPPE STARCK, THE RESTAURANT IS LOCATED IN AN OPEN SPACE COMPOSED OF SEVERAL AREAS DEFINED BY THEIR USE OF COLOR AND FURNITURE.

The Patisserie and Chocolate Room are paradise for gourmands. Traditional and innovative tapas are served on a cart that is pushed around the bar.

Casa Lever

This restaurant is located on the ground floor of the hallmark fifties building Lever House, designed by Gordon Bunshaft, near Grand Central Terminal. The current establishment is a reopening of the work by well-known entrepreneurs Gherardo Guarducci and Dimitri Pauli, from the Sant Ambroeus chain.

The wooden-clad walls and ceilings are reminiscent of a spaceship. With the refurbishment, the space has a warmer feeling thanks to the Venini glass chandeliers, the red tables, and carpets.

The Studio 54–style Andy Warhol copies belong to the restaurant and the collector Aby Rosen. Opposite, the wine shelves that divide the booths on the west side reflect light, creating a pleasant ambience. The Italian-inspired food has made a name for itself among connoisseurs.

Designer: MARC NEWSON (INTERIOR)
www.casalever.com
Location: NEW YORK, NY, USA
Opening date: OCTOBER 2009
Photos: © WHITNEY COX

CASA LEVER BRINGS ITALIAN CUISINE WITH A MODERN SENSIBILITY INTO THE DESIGN OF THE ICONIC LEVER HOUSE, MAKING IT A WORTHY SPOT BURSTING WITH PURE NEW YORK SOPHISTICATION.

Classic New York-style art is featured on the restaurant's east-side wall.

Mercat a la Planxa

The spirit of Barcelona comes alive in this venue located in the Blackstone Hotel on Michigan Avenue in Chicago. Its aim is to bring the buzz from the vibrant meat, fruit, and vegetable markets in the Catalan capital to downtown Chicago.

The bar located at the entrance and covered in walnut is reminiscent of a classic Spanish bar. The rear of its space is surrounded by a curved screen composed of hexagonal blocks in multiple colors which enclose the staircase.

The restaurant's dining room is distributed over the second and third floor. A series of large-format illustrations of street life in Barcelona were applied to the glass and mirrors. Bright fuchsia, green upholstery, and tiled floors contrast with the more classic style of the hotel. From the large open-plan kitchen, the specialties of the house, mainly tapas, are served by award-winning chef Jose Garces.

Designer: D-ASH DESIGN
www.mercatchicago.com
Location: CHICAGO, IL, USA
Opening date: MARCH 2008
Photos: © FRANK OUDEMAN

IN THE DESIGN OF THIS RESTAURANT, THE ARCHITECTS USED SPANISH MODERN DESIGN ELEMENTS TO CREATE A VIBRANT ATMOSPHERE REMINISCENT OF THE FAMOUS BUSTLING FOOD MARKETS IN BARCELONA.

The restaurant is spread over three floors; all floors enjoy views of the city through the large windows of the building.

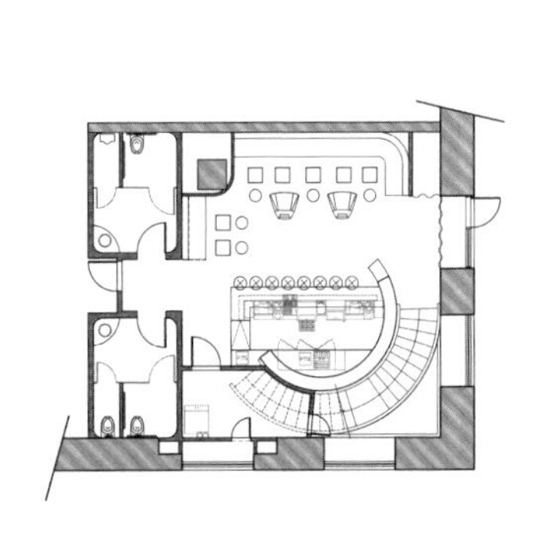

First floor plan

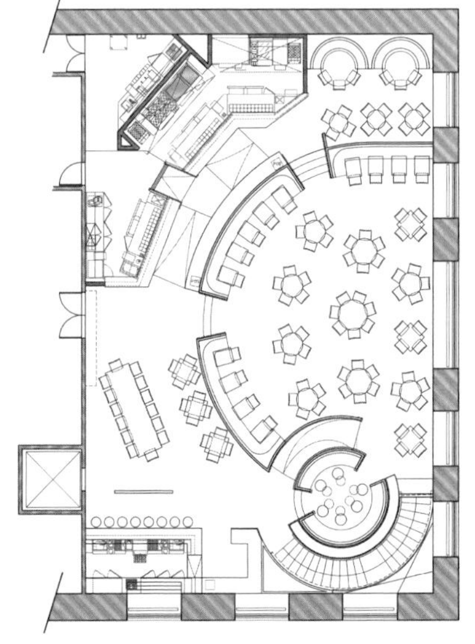

Second floor plan

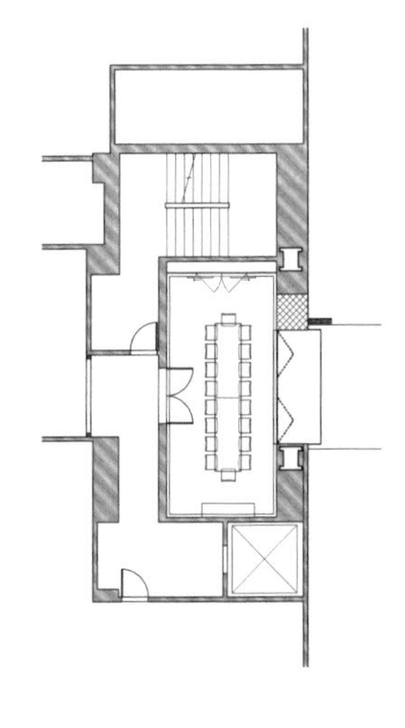

Thrid floor plan

Bar Astrid y Gastón

This bar was renovated to look like the restaurant it is a part of, although its shape, orientation, and general characteristics are unique. Its shape is that of an irregular polyhedron, a design idea generated from a detailed study on the dimensions of the space available for the restaurant. The upper area of the polyhedron derives its shape from a metal covering perforated with a geometric pattern from a laser cutter. This gives patrons a feeling of being underneath the shade of a vine arbor.

The ceiling of the bar creates an atmosphere that works both during the day and in the evening. The organic form of the bar itself brings the restaurant's various spatial geometries together, and directs patrons' attention to a bench running all the way around the bar where they can sit and relax with their beverages. There is also a large horizontal opening for those who wish to enjoy the outdoor terrace.

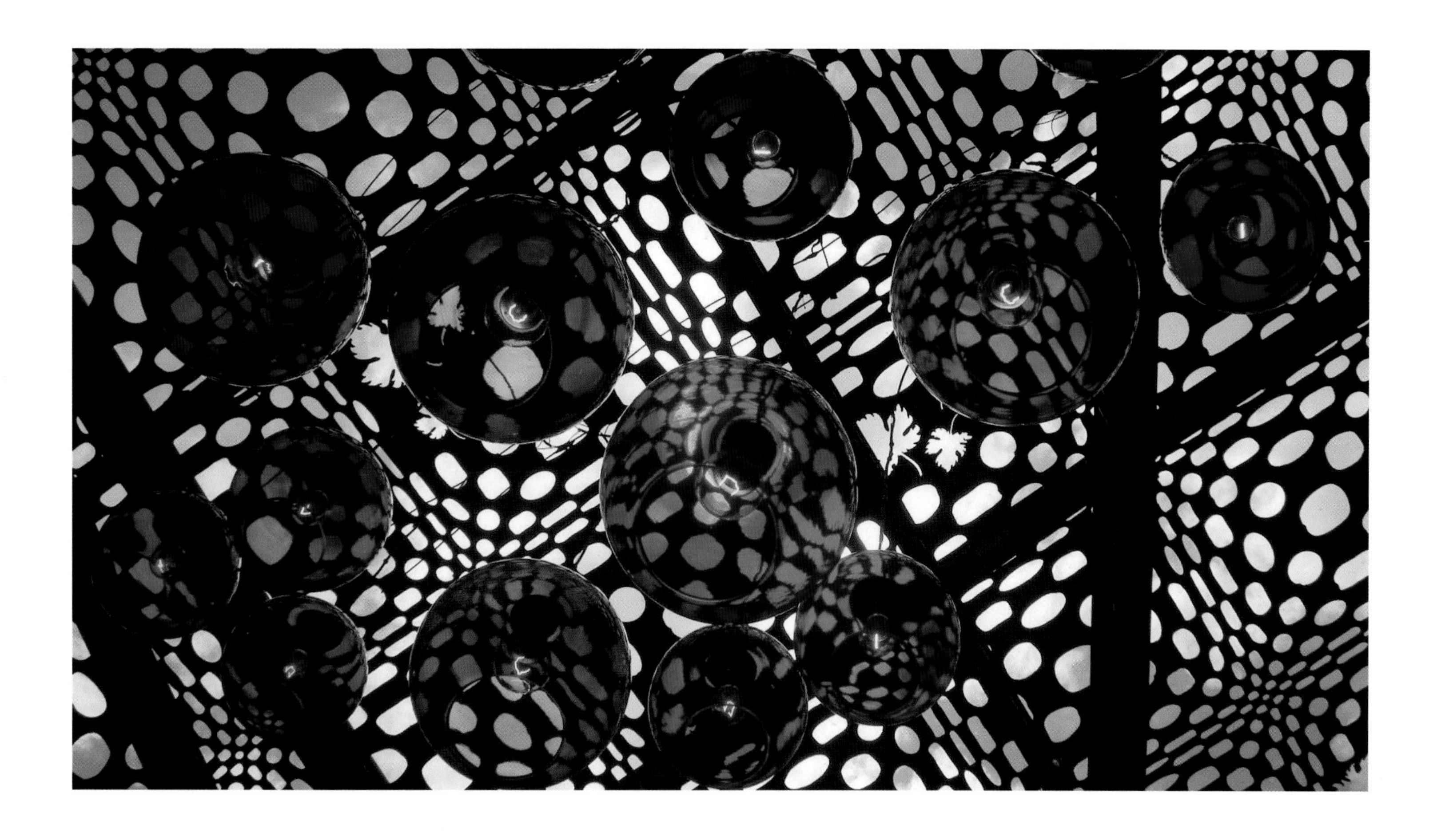

Designer: MANUEL VILLA
Associate Architect: PAULA CASTRO
www.astridygaston.com
Location: BOGOTÁ, COLOMBIA
Opening date: NOVEMBER 2008
Photos: © MANUEL VILLA, LAURA RICO, MATEO FOLADOR

THE PERFORATED METAL SHEETING COVERING THE CEILING OF THE BAR CREATES A LIGHT AND SHADE EFFECT THAT CONJURES UP THE FEELING OF BEING UNDERNEATH A VINE ARBOR.

The bar occupies the old garage and rear courtyard of the building where the restaurant is now.

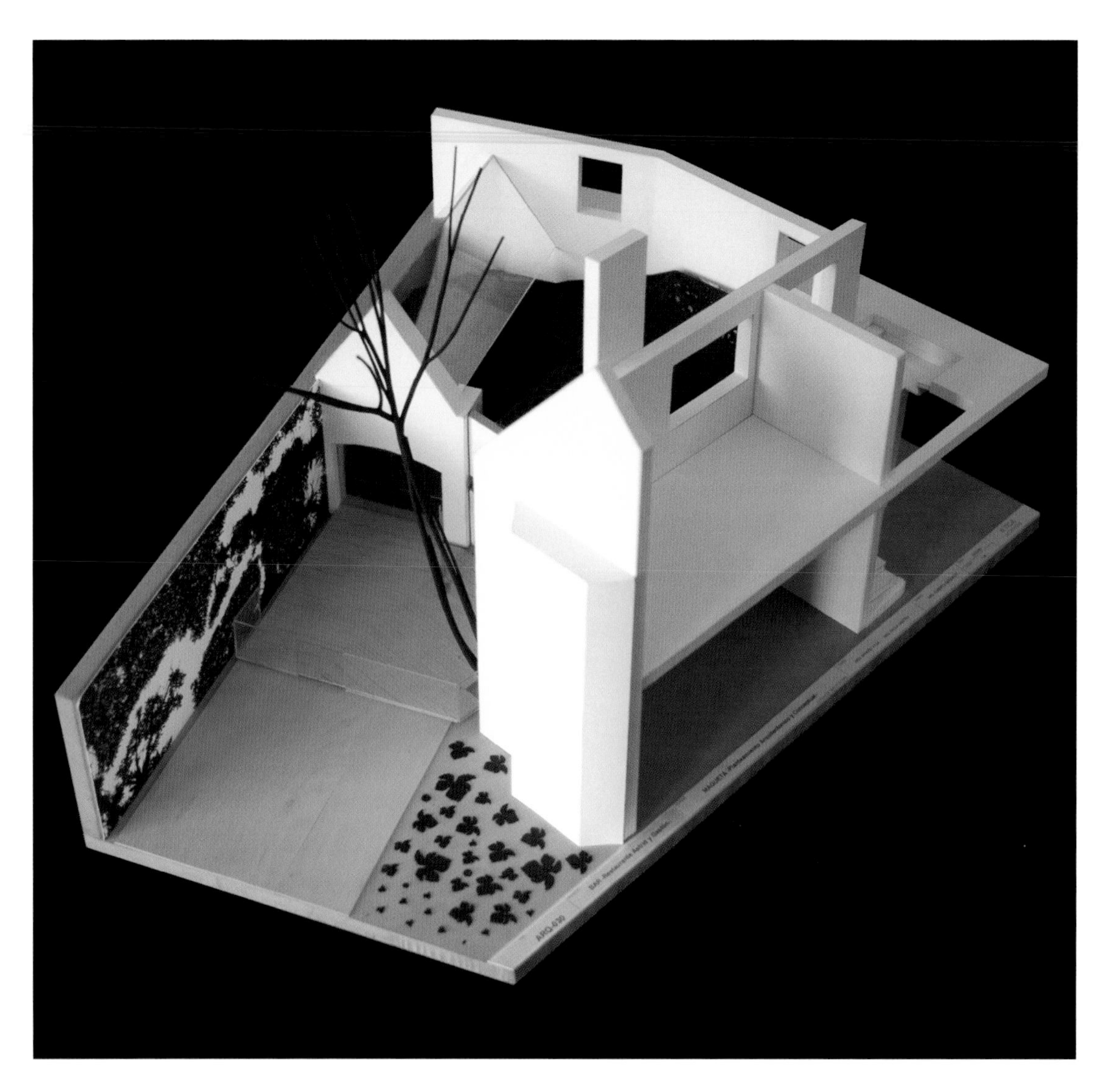

Model

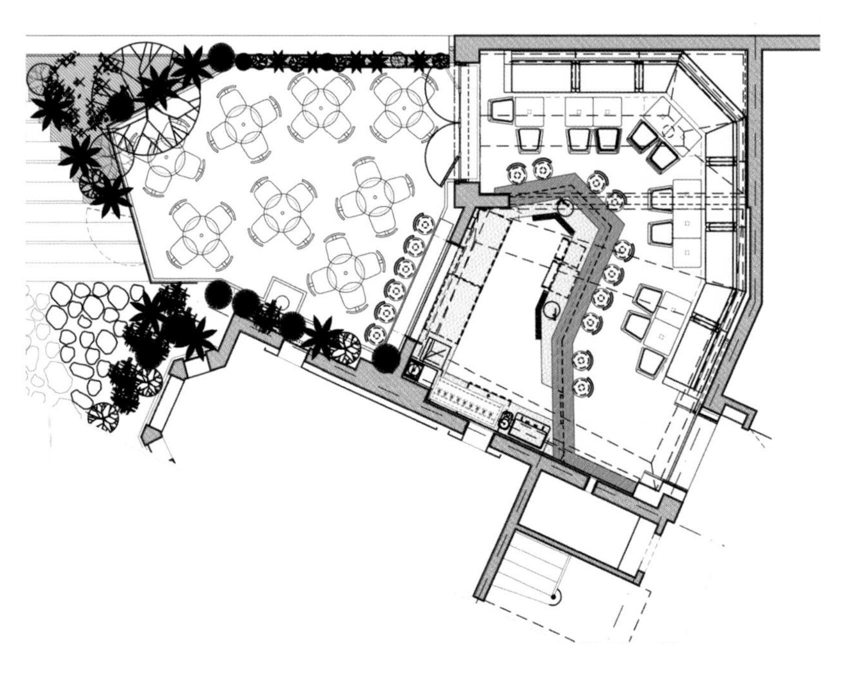

Floor plan

PARIS
SÃO PAULO
LONDON

Forneria San Paolo

The minimalist design of the space occupied by this restaurant lends itself to an interesting interplay of architectural forms, materials, and transparencies. The wooden elements play a key role in creating a warm, cozy atmosphere. The paneling on the walls lends a certain unity to the different areas of the restaurant, and establishes a visual link with the ceiling, which is made of slender strips of wood. The floor is covered with tiny colored square cobblestones placed together to resemble a mosaic.

The kitchen opens out into the main dining area, separated from it by only a glass partition covered with a special film that makes its surface seem either frosted or completely transparent depending on the angle from which it is viewed. Decorative details range from the copper light fixtures designed by Tom Dixon to the 15 George Nelson clocks from the 1950s and '60s, which were reissued by Vitra.

Designer: STUDIO MK27
Location: SÃO PAULO, BRAZIL
Opening date: JANUARY 2009
Photos: © RÔMULO FIALDINI

USING THE CONCEPT OF AN OPEN KITCHEN, THE CHEFS CAN BE SEEN AT WORK FROM ALL PARTS OF THE RESTAURANT THROUGH THE GLASS PARTITION SEPARATING THE KITCHEN FROM THE DINING AREA.

The floor consists of numerous pieces of marble—each of which is one square centimeter in size. Tables were specially made for the restaurant. Chairs have leather upholstery.

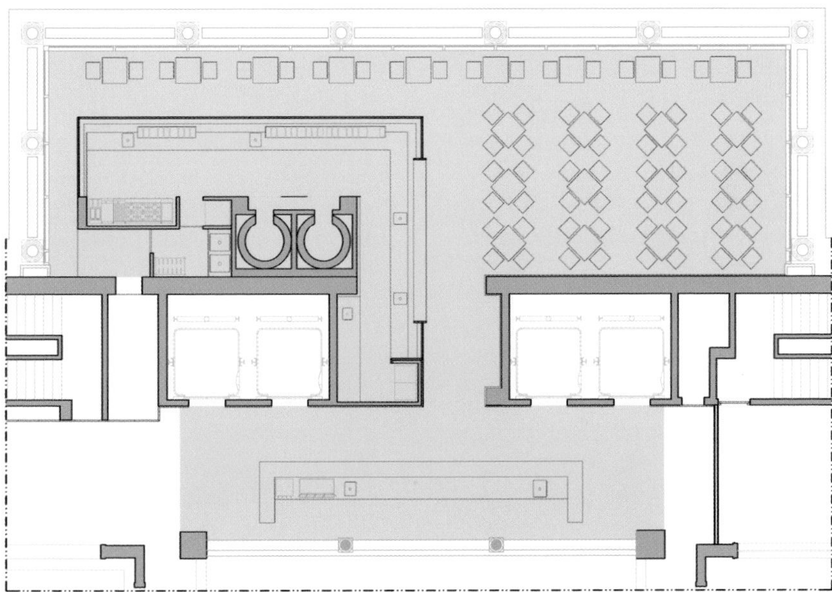

Floor plan

FORNERIA SAN PAOLO

Asia & Oceania

Hoto Fudo

Viewed from afar, this restaurant's building looks like an igloo, a cloud, or a tent at the foot of Mount Fuji. It is actually a noodle restaurant, which combines traditional Japanese decor with industrial materials to create a space where there is not a single straight line or edge in sight.

The building is an undulating concrete structure on steel mesh. It has openings in its walls so that fresh air circulates in and out of the restaurant; at times, this brings moisture into the restaurant. Its acrylic doors are rarely used and frequently remain wide open, thereby reinforcing the feeling of open space.

The minimalist interior resembles a school cafeteria, with long wooden tables and benches that are randomly positioned throughout the space. The openings in the walls guarantee visual contact with nature. An exterior layer of insulating material helps to maintain stable temperatures in the interior and enhance the shape of the building.

Designer: TAKESHI HOSAKA ARCHITECTS
Location: YAMANASHI, JAPAN
Opening date: DECEMBER 2009
Photos: © KOJI FUJI/NACASA & PARTNERS

THE DESIGN ALLOWS RAIN AND FOG TO ENTER THROUGH OPENINGS IN THE WALLS, AND THE WIND TO CIRCULATE INSIDE.

In line with traditional Japanese design, the restaurant features clean lines and bare spaces.

不動

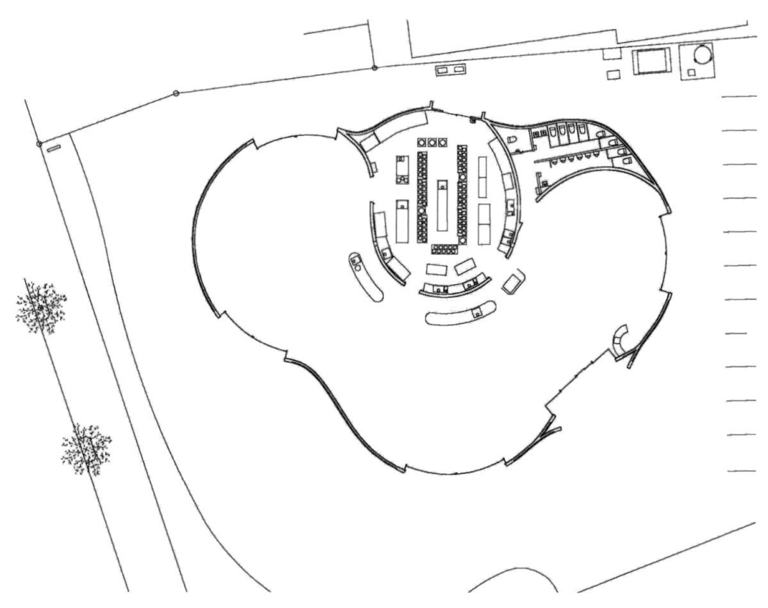

Site plan

Nautilus Project

This restaurant is located on the fourth floor of a new mall in Singapore, the ION Orchard. The establishment is owned by the president of a freight shipping company, and the kitchen is run by well-known chef Jason Dell, a specialist in cooking seafood.

Its semicurved plan led the architects to implement curved wooden surfaces and to form booths with different uses. Flat wooden-paneled walls decorate the kitchen. Semitransparent surfaces consisting of slats of wood outline semiprivate spaces that can accommodate a small table for two or a larger table for ten. Marine-inspired oval shapes are repeated in the windows of the semi-interior spaces, and in the ceiling through openings that look like skylights.

Designer: DESIGN SPIRITS
www.thenautilusproject.com
Location: SINGAPORE, SINGAPORE
Opening date: OCTOBER 2009
Photos: © TOSHIHIKO KAJIHARA

ORGANIC FORMS THAT REPRESENT PORTHOLES TO THE SEABED DEFINE THE CHARACTER OF THIS RESTAURANT SPECIALIZING IN SEAFOOD, WHOSE OWNER IS THE DIRECTOR OF A SHIPPING COMPANY.

The curves that dominate the space are an extension of the plan of the restaurant.

EXIT
S&S

Pearls & Caviar

This restaurant, part of Abu Dhabi's Shangri-La Hotel, occupies a separate building beside the river. Its design represents a fusion of East and West, with a nexus of luxury. Traditional Oriental shapes and materials were reconceived in black-and-white abstract forms.

The restaurant is divided into two areas that give the venue its name. The "pearl" section was designed in white and silver and occupies a terrace on level one. It has an area reserved for private use, as well as a circular bar and a lounge protected from the strong sunlight by canvas sails.

The "caviar" area was designed in black and silver hues and is more intimate. It has a mosaic on the floor that simulates a huge Arabian carpet, as well as sections featuring various different ambiences created by partitions made of metallic chain curtains. The bar furnishings are made of stainless steel and black marble. Its circular seats are covered in leather.

Designer: CONCRETE
www.pearlsandcaviar.com
Location: ABU DHABI, UNITED ARAB EMIRATES
Opening date: JULY 2008
Photos: © RICHARD THORN

THE ARCHITECTS DESIGNED EVERYTHING FROM THE LOGO, BUSINESS CARDS, AND WEB SITE TO THE CUTLERY, STAFF UNIFORMS, INTERIOR DÉCOR, AND LANDSCAPING.

The mosaics on the floor of the terrace and restaurant simulate Oriental carpets, albeit with a range of hues in keeping with each specific environment.

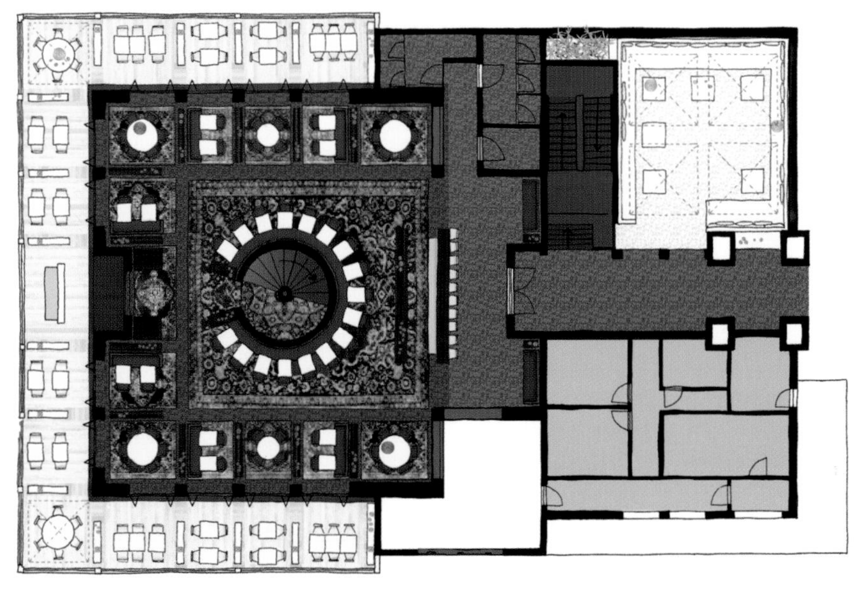

Floor plan

Urbane

The Urbane restaurant has always been a culinary reference in Brisbane, having won a number of prizes for the quality of its food. Recent architectural work expanded the restaurant and allowed it to add three additional areas for dining and drinking. Today, high-quality fare continues to be served at Urbane; Sub-Urbane is a winery and restaurant with stone walls dating back one hundred years; Euro is a bistro; and The Laneway is a bar.

The new spaces are arranged around the kitchen, which was made much bigger. This center of operations for the restaurant can now cater for up to three hundred diners and accommodate up to thirty chefs during peak hours.

Each dining area was designed in accordance with its own idiosyncrasies in terms of materials, lighting, and furniture. The different atmospheres are connected by a number of doors, some of which are open, while others are gateways to more private areas. These are opened and shut as need dictates, for the various events organized at the venue.

Designer: ARKHEFIELD
www.urbanerestaurant.com
Location: BRISBANE, AUSTRALIA
Opening date: NOVEMBER 2009
Photos: © SCOTT BURROWS

THANKS TO THE FOUR SPACES, WHICH ARE SEPARATE AREAS AS FAR AS STYLE AND SERVICES ARE CONCERNED, THE RESTAURANT HAS STRENGTHENED ITS PRIVILEGED POSITION IN THE CULINARY WORLD OF BRISBANE.

To maintain unique identities for each space, an effort was made to keep each one's range of colors, style of furniture, and even key materials different from the others.

BSmith
Herd 2009

THRONG
KEEP
LANEWAY
DO NOT
TURN
SLIPPERY
STOP
GIVE
HEAD
WAY
BACK
MERGE

U: Ponte Vecchio

The menu of this upscale restaurant offers Italian cuisine, but the style of eating is Japanese, and patrons enjoy their food with chopsticks. The visual identity of the establishment is also different from traditional Italian restaurants that try to recreate the ambience of *trattorias*. Instead of using traditional Italian design, its design is modern and simple.

The restaurant is organized around a U-shaped counter that creates a space for meeting and exchanges. Its lighting plan follows the shape of the bar, using overhead lights and a screen with a gold graphic pattern that contrasts with the prevailing tone of the room. Because the architects wanted to add an air of mystery, they decorated the interior in black and granite tones that stand out against the silver and red surfaces formed by the restaurant's mosaic tiles.

Designer: NIKKEN SEKKEI
www.ponte-vecchio.co.jp
Location: OSAKA, JAPAN
Opening date: MAY 2008
Photos: © NACASA & PARTNERS

LOCATED IN THE CITY OF OSAKA, JAPAN, U: PONTE VECCHIO IS A RESTAURANT WITH ITALIAN CUISINE, BUT JAPANESE STYLE; PASTA AND RISOTTOS ARE EATEN WITH CHOPSTICKS.

The seats around the bar and tables are a unique aesthetic element of the décor.

Bommie Restaurant

Inspired by the colors of the Coral Sea in the Pacific Ocean, marine life, and the outline of vessels, the Hamilton Island Yacht Club is a local icon. An undulating copper roof encases three levels of facilities, including the Bommie Restaurant—the interior of which was entirely designed by the architect, from the joinery, to the tables, the selection of furniture, the lighting, and the tableware.

The interior of the restaurant has a design sequence that ends in a raised platform in the central dining room. The roof is made from perforated plywood panels, and is inspired by images of soaring silhouettes with full sails. The filigree metal that goes up to the ceiling and the fishing nets are the work of sculptor Glenn Murray. The marine ambience is complemented by lighting fixtures that resemble buoys gently floating in space.

Designer: WALTER BARDA DESIGN
www.hamiltonislandyachtclub.com.au
Location: HAMILTON ISLAND, AUSTRALIA
Opening date: NOVEMBER 2009
Photos: © CIARAN HANDY

FORMS AND MATERIALS REPRESENTING THE WORLD OF NAVIGATION ARE THE HALLMARK OF THIS RESTAURANT LOCATED IN AN EXCLUSIVE YACHT CLUB OF THE AUSTRALIAN ISLANDS ON THE CORAL SEA.

The three-sided tables bear the name "Periwinkle," and were specially designed to fit the curved outline of the restaurant.

The Tote

This bar and restaurant evolved as a result of reconverting an old colonial building, where bets used to be placed, at the Royal Western India Turf Club. In compliance with local regulations governing conservation issues, three quarters of the building had to respect the original style of the roof. The remaining quarter had to be maintained as it was.

The building is located in the middle of a dense grove of trees that seem to have invaded its interior, so that the structural framework mimics the branches of a tree. The space houses a wine bar, restaurant, and banquet hall, each with a different structure of branches. Holes were perforated in the ceiling between spaces left by the intersections of the structural branches to let light in.

The interior of the lounge bar is distinguished by a three-dimensional wooden panel, which was treated to be sound absorbing. Its framework is a series of trees with intertwined branches.

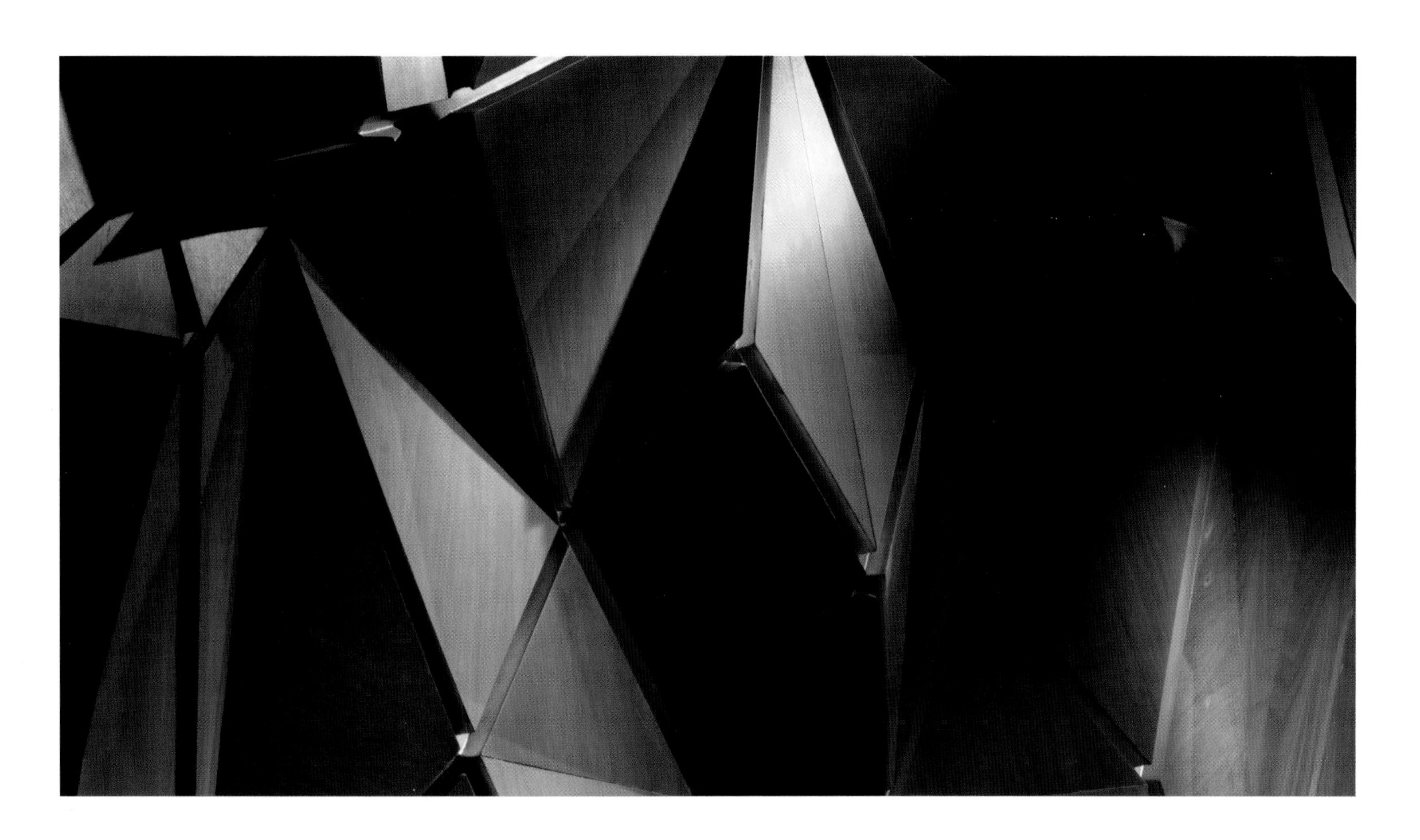

Designer: CHRIS LEE AND KAPIL GUPTA/SERIE ARCHITECTS
Location: MUMBAI, INDIA
Opening date: OCTOBER 2009
Photos: © EDMUND SUMNER

THE OLD BUILDING, WHERE BETS USED TO BE PLACED ON RACING HORSES, WAS CONVERTED INTO A RESTAURANT AND BAR WITH A STRUCTURE THAT APPEARS AS A PROLONGATION OF THE HUGE GROVE OF TREES SURROUNDING IT.

The false ceiling, made of panels and plasterboard, houses an intricate lighting system that offers a variety of ways to showcase the space depending on the type of event organized.

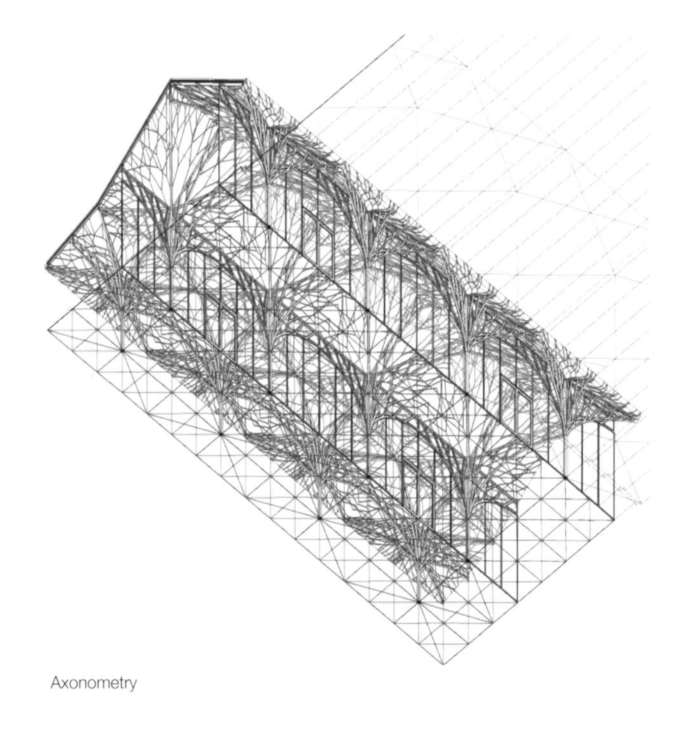

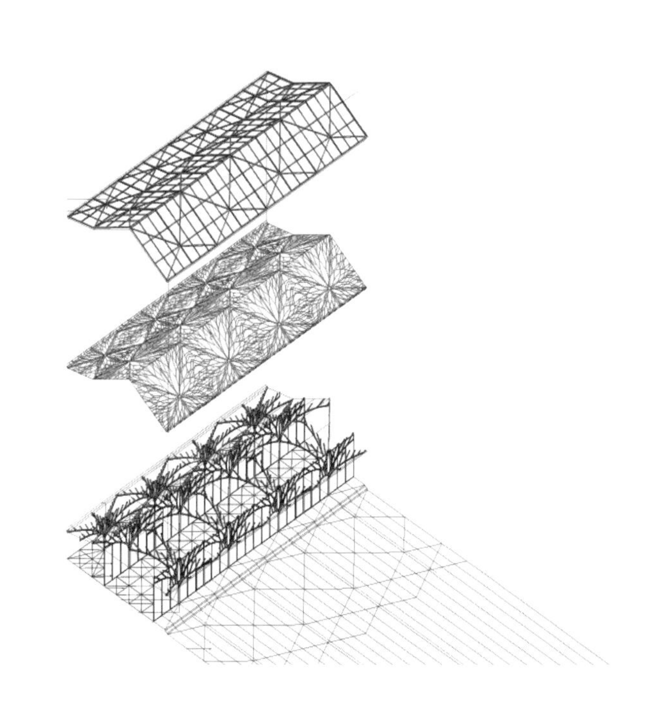

Axonometry

I-T.Alia

Historical links between India and Italy have been taken into account in the design of this space. The ancient Roman ships that used the monsoons to cross the Indian Ocean to trade spices, precious stones, ivory and gold, have inspired the interior design, which references to the exotic spices and attractive precious metals.

A bronze totem seated opposite a curved wall clad in oak welcomes diners. The café, located to its right, has a relaxed atmosphere, with white-painted brick, wooden beams, and tiled flooring. Here, a display counter exhibits special dishes and their ingredients. The terrace can be accessed from this space.

The restaurant and the bar are to the left of the entrance. The bar appears to float opposite a panel of gold mosaic tiles. Its curve is reproduced on the screen of metallic lines that separates it from the dining room.

Designer: PROJECT ORANGE
Location: DELHI, INDIA
Opening date: FEBRUARY 2009
Photos: © ALI RANGOONWALA

THE ARCHITECTS HAVE WORKED WITH TWO MAIN FOCUS POINTS—GLAMOUR AND RUSTIC SIMPLICITY—TO CREATE AN ENVIRONMENT THAT IS TRUE TO THE ROOTS OF ITALIAN CUISINE BUT ALSO IS ORIGINAL.

The polished stone floor reflects the gold glitter in the restaurant; the ceiling follows the shape of the bar, and is highlighted with the use of lighting.

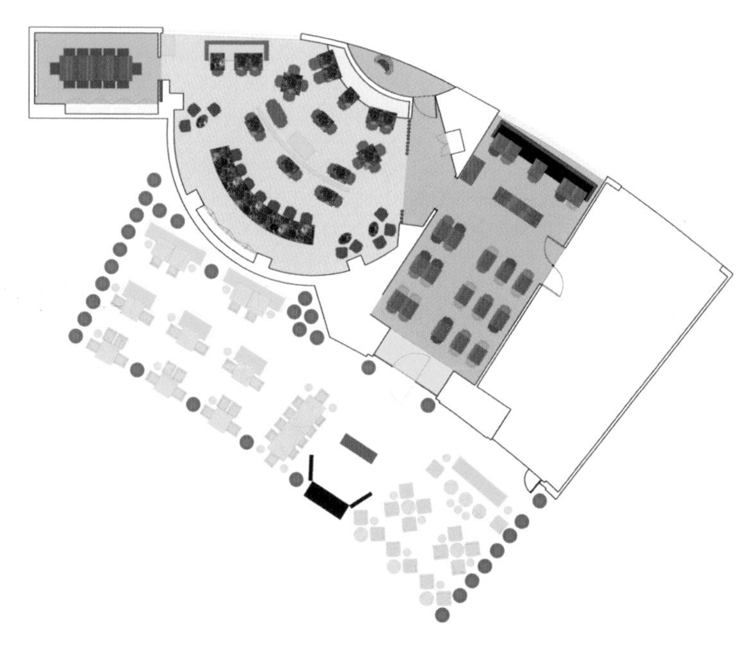

Floor plan

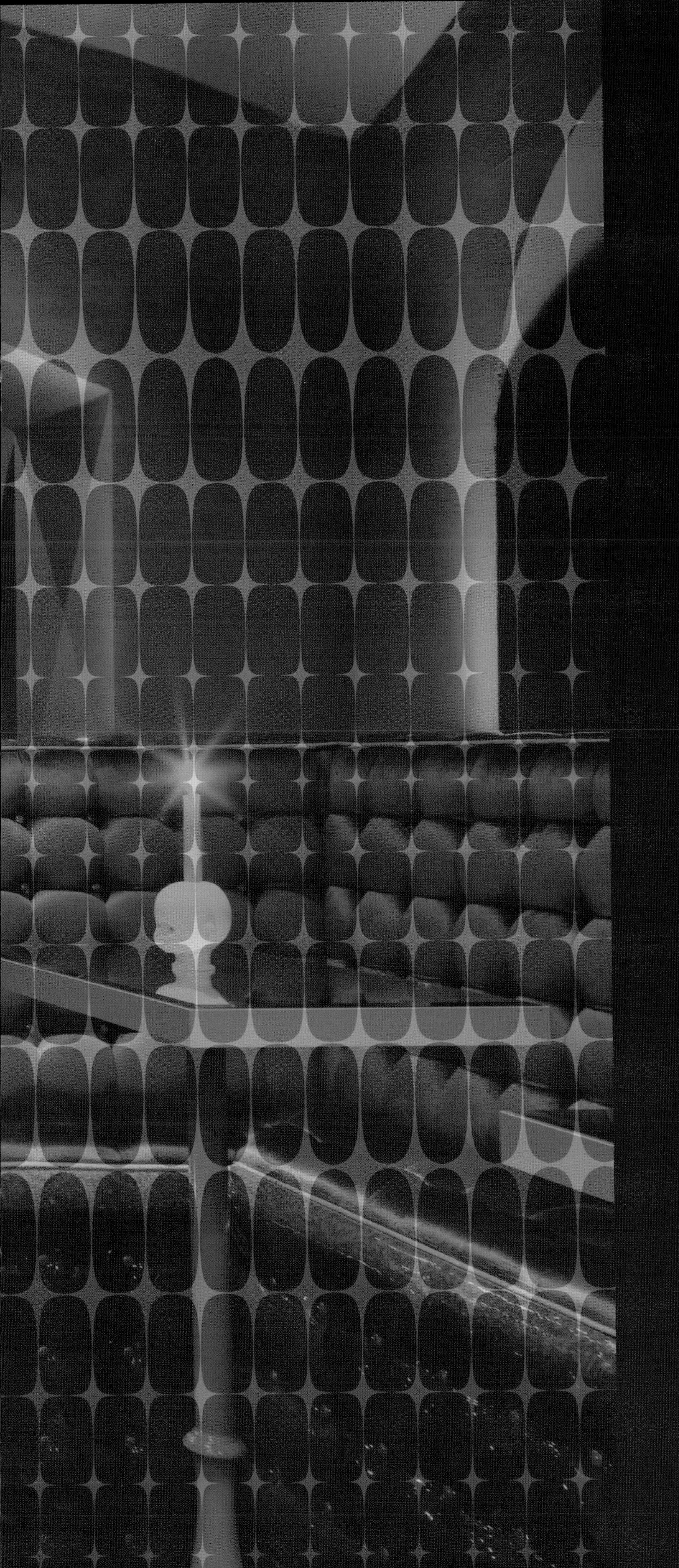

Europe

TRUSSARDI
TRUSSARDI
DAL 1911

Café Trussardi

Located in the pedestrian precinct of the charming Piazza Ferrari (a stone throw away from Piazza della Scala) in the heart of Milan, the bar and restaurant of the Trussardi fashion house rises before visitors like an unexpected garden—appearing like a glass box with a "green cloud" floating above it. The glass box, which is entirely transparent, reveals a bar and restaurant designed to reflect the historical origins of Palazzo Trussardi, which date back to 1911. Inside its café are large leather-backed chairs designed by Pantone. The "green cloud" is, in fact, large vertical gardens designed by Patrick Blanc and planted on panels both inside and outside of the premises. Five square yards of greenery were planted for every car that used to park in the Piazza. The kitchen, which serves Mediterranean and Italian fare, is run by award-winning Michelin Chef Andrea Berton.

Designer: CARLO RATTI ASSOCIATI, WALTER NICOLINO & CARLO RATTI WITH PATRICK BLANC
www.trussardi.com
Location: MILAN, ITALY
Opening date: APRIL 2008
Photos: © PINO DELL'AQUILA, MAX TOMASINELLI, WALTER NICOLINO

MORE THAN 120 PLANT SPECIES MAKE UP THE GARDENS TOPPING THE GLASS STRUCTURE OF IL RISTORANTE TRUSSARDI ALLA SCALA.

The irrigation and drainage pipes converge in four very slender columns on their way to an underground cistern.

0-24

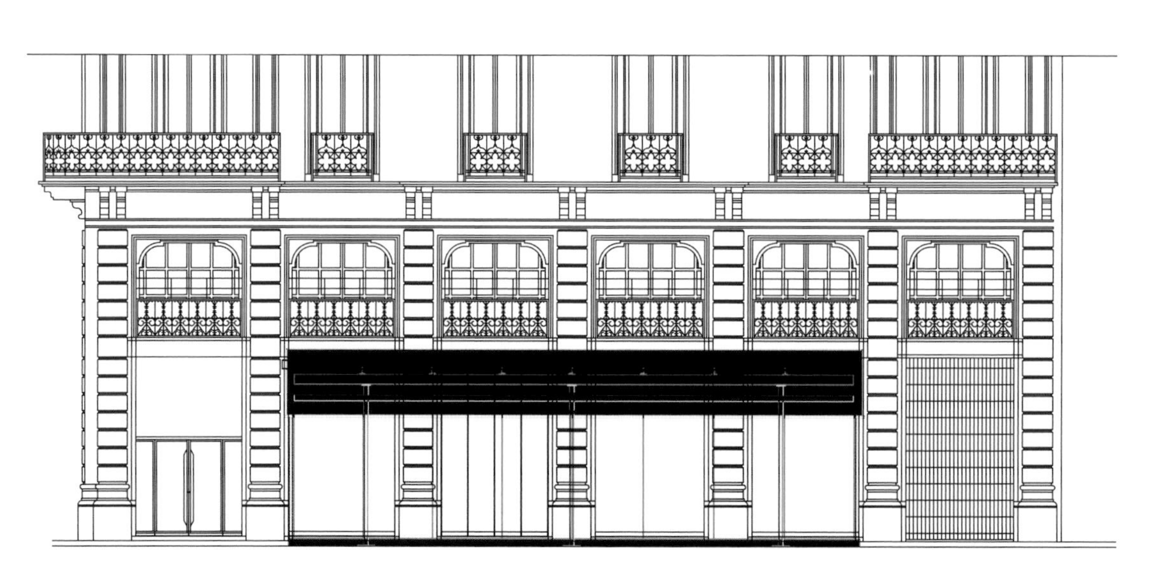

Elevation

de Bijenkorf Kitchen

The cuisine offered at this restaurant in Amsterdam's de Bijenkorf department store draws on gastronomic traditions from around the world. For this reason, the extensive shelving skirting the premises is not only used for storage space, but also to showcase the restaurant's large range of ingredients from different countries.

The restaurant, which is located in the center of the building, is divided into two sides. On one side, five buffets offer hot dishes; on the other side, three islands offer cold dishes and beverages.

The dining area is divided into two zones: one bathed in light, thanks to the large windows in the ceiling and sides of the room, and another more modest and intimate area. Both areas were built using the same materials, but with different finishes and furnishings. The floors and tables are made of different shades of bamboo. The seats range from high chairs at the bar to sofas in the lounge area.

Designer: CONCRETE
www.bijenkorf.nl
Location: AMSTERDAM, THE NETHERLANDS
Opening date: JULY 2008
Photos: © EWOUT HUIBERS

PASTRY

ACCORDING TO THE ARCHITECTS, "SINCE THE RESTAURANT IS LOCATED IN A DEPARTMENT STORE, THE FOCUS IS PRIMARILY ON THE RAW MATERIALS AND THE FOOD."

Bags of rice from Indonesia, fresh herbs from Vietnam, and cans of oil and dried tomatoes from Tuscany are just some of the ingredients on display.

Stainless steel and anthracite were used throughout the hot buffet areas. Bamboo and black natural stones were used in the island areas, reserved for cold dishes.

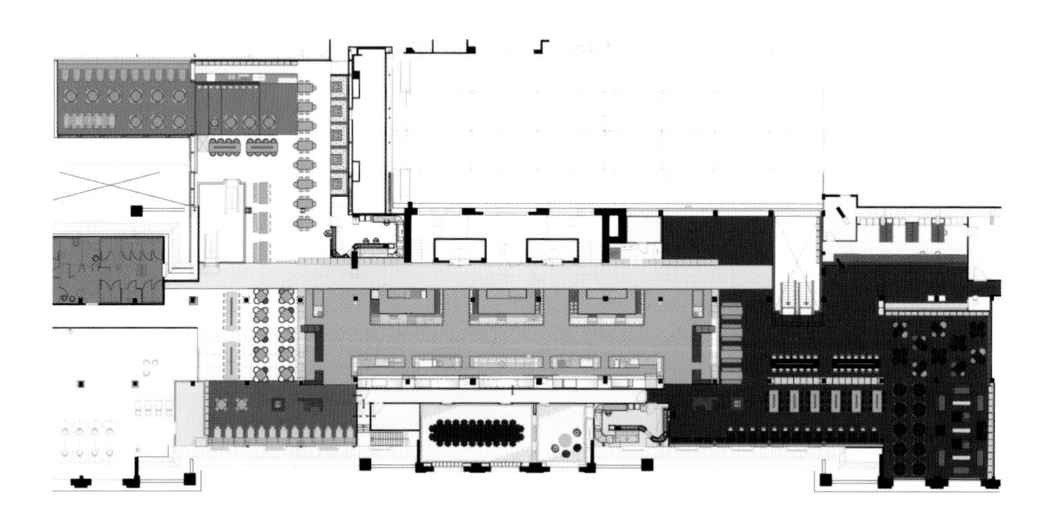

Floor plan

ITALIAN
JUICE

door

DAM
CAFÉ B
4

Estado Puro

The sensitivity of famous Spanish chef Paco Roncero toward modern cuisine provided the starting point for the architects of this restaurant to create a space in which tradition and innovation converge. The result: a gorgeous tapas bar with a privileged location on the famous Paseo del Prado boulevard and a terrace on the street.

The architects' design allows the wall and ceiling to run together, using the same material: a skin featuring an ornamental comb that is repeated over and over again. This comb, which is typical of Spanish folklore and often sold as a souvenir, thus takes on a new dimension that is sophisticated and chic. Its design transcends its architectural function to adopt a role in promoting the image of the restaurant.

Another focus of attention is the main bar—a huge piece of marble in its raw state, bereft of any treatment since it left the quarry—and the baskets on the secondary bars which hold produce reserved for "show cooking."

Designer: JAMES & MAU
www.tapasenestadopuro.com
Location: MADRID, SPAIN
Opening date: SUMMER 2009
Photos: © JAVIER PEÑAS

FEMININE, ELEGANT, AND VERY SHOWY, THE REINVENTED ORNAMENTAL COMB HAS NOW BECOME AN ICON OF THIS RESTAURANT RUN BY ONE OF THE MOST INNOVATIVE CHEFS IN SPAIN.

A thousand ornamental combs give shape to a backlit area of the wall and ceiling, appearing on top of one another as if they were the scales of a fish.

SXXI
BOCADILLOS Y ENSALADAS

La Xina

Textures, colors, aromas, steam from the kitchens, the patina of aged wood, wall lamps in the form of Chinese lanterns, and the symbolism of the dragon lamp, all help to create a Chinese feel in this restaurant without falling into the trap of clichés. Wood, thought of as a sophisticated material, is the predominant element. For the wall cladding and to separate some of the spaces, Chinese wooden lattices were used. The floor is aged oak.

The restaurant's warm lighting highlights key areas and creates intimate spaces within it. The kitchen has a special lighting system to bring the work of the chefs to the foreground. Close to the facade and hovering above a long red table, a large parchment dragon hangs from the ceiling. It creates a visual connection with the second floor. The upper level is home to a large bar with a kitchen. The third and last space is a loft with a modern adaptation of different-sized Chinese lanterns.

Designer: SANDRA TARRUELLA INTERIORISTAS
www.grupotragaluz.com
Location: BARCELONA, SPAIN
Opening date: APRIL 2008
Photos: © OLGA PLANAS

LA★XINA
RESTAURANT
ORIENTAL
BARCELONA
TRAGALUZ

THE OPEN-PLAN KITCHEN, WHERE DINERS CAN WATCH THEIR MEALS BEING PREPARED, AND THE SHARED TABLES REINFORCE THE SOCIAL ASPECT OF FOOD, WHICH IS EXTREMELY IMPORTANT IN CHINA.

The kitchen occupies a central location to provide the entertainment of watching how meals are made.

Pioneer
Pioneer

Whisky Mist at Zeta

The name for this bar, which is located on the old site of the Zeta Bar, has two associations: the drink that is a part of its name and the favorite deer of Queen Victoria. Its design—a glamorous, dark, and sparkling atmosphere with luxurious finishes and reflective surfaces—is an abstract reference to the drink.

The architects attempted to avoid anything vulgar, traditional, or too overtly related to whiskey. Thus the interior is the archetype of sophistication, with a palette dominated almost exclusively by shades of black and gold, and a graphic identity that represents the reflections of amber-colored whiskey in a clear glass. The space is composed of the main bar, the VIP lounge, and a dance floor surrounded by mirrors. The ceiling features a grid of LED lights.

Designer: BLACKSHEEP
www.whiskymist.com
Location: LONDON, UK
Opening date: SUMMER 2008
Photos: © INGRID RASMUSSEN

PANELS OF BLACK WITH EMBOSSED OCTAGONAL SHAPES ARE FEATURED IN THE ENTRANCE LOBBY AND BAR. A REFERENCE TO SCOTLAND—THE LAND OF WHISKEY—THE PANELS USE A DECORATIVE DETAIL THAT IS COMMON IN SCOTTISH CASTLES.

The front of the bar has the cladding, with a "zebra-skin effect" similar to the front entrance. The counter of the bar is lit up and reminiscent of whiskey.

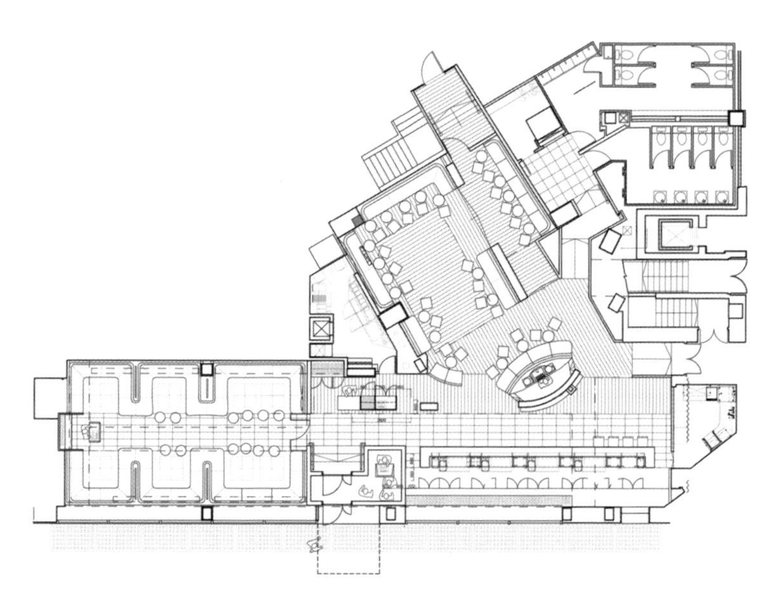

Floor plan

Ristorante Olivomare

References to the maritime world are no accident in this restaurant, which specializes in Italian cooking using products from the sea. Its most explicit feature is unquestionably the wall in its main dining room, which features a fish print inspired by the drawings of M. C. Escher. As a visual counterpoint to this, there are hundreds of nylon tubes hanging in spirals from the ceiling in a linear sequence (Bigoli lights, made by Innermost), and appearing like jellyfish or sea anemones. Where these are located is also the place of the bar, which features a countertop made of Corian.

In addition to the main dining area, there is a second one of smaller dimensions located at the back of the restaurant. With an enormous skylight, its curved walls have an embossed texture reminiscent of beach sand that has been fashioned into shapes and clusters by the wind. There is also a door here leading to a small lounge for the restrooms. The door is decorated with the tentacles of tangled coral. This design, also used on the washbasins, is in deep contrast to the pure, unadulterated white of the dining room.

Designer: PIERLUIGI PIU
www.olivorestaurants.com
Location: LONDON, UK
Opening date: MAY 2007
Photos: © GIORGIO DETTORI, PIERLUIGI PIU

THE INTERIOR OF THIS SEAFOOD RESTAURANT IN ENGLAND'S DISTRICT OF BELGRAVIA WAS CREATED TO REFLECT THE SEA WORLD THROUGH THE USE OF MODERN ART AND CONTEMPORARY DESIGN.

Tables are the Dizzie model and were made by Arper. The Lago chairs were designed by Philippe Starck for Driade.

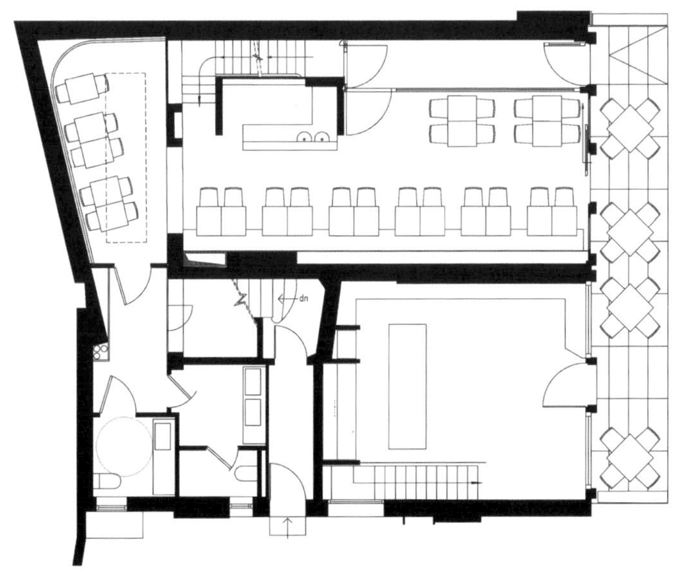

Floor plan

PASTILLES

Les Pastilles

This extraordinary place, which is very different from normal run-of-the-mill restaurants, is located in Cap 3000, one of the oldest shopping malls in France. Its designers shaped its space to appear like a number of small village squares, in which people can get together and socialize in a relaxed manner.

Located in the middle of the ground floor of the mall, the venue looks like an island with interconnected archipelagos. But the designers purposefully planned Les Pastilles to be a protected area, offering privacy in spite of its open layout. Its architectural elements and ornamental discs were arranged to cater to different states of mind; the outer tables are ideal for a quick snack break between purchases, whereas tables located closer to the center of the restaurant and larger in size tempt occupants to stay longer. Corner tables have booths with fringed curtains offering greater privacy.

Designer: MATALI CRASSET
www.cap3000.com
Location: NICE, FRANCE
Opening date: JULY 2009
Photos: © JÉRÔME SPRIET, NICOLAS CALLUAUD

LOCATED IN A SHOPPING MALL, LES PASTILLES IS A UNIVERSE MADE UP OF SEVERAL INTERCONNECTED SPACES DESIGNED TO OFFER OPTIONS FOR LEISURE OR PRIVACY OR BOTH, IN ACCORDANCE WITH THE NEEDS OF ITS PATRONS.

All areas of the restaurant have the same shade of fuchsia on the floor and are connected by an interlocking metallic structure that forms part of a huge circle.

nice-matin

ODC

Orlando di Castello Restaurant

This restaurant was designed with the idea of bringing together influences as far apart as Queen Elizabeth, rap, and Tyrol, which is located in west Austria. Thus, elements such as delicate floral arrangements and metal light fittings are repeated throughout the premises, making the use of contrast a key design feature of the restaurant.

Baseboards are wall cladding, table lamps were converted into ceiling lights, and seats are divided into small kidney-shaped pieces. Ironic upsets make for a surrealist atmosphere.

The use of a wide range of furniture differentiates between the different areas of the restaurant. Carefully designed lighting helps to create "micro-climates." The restaurant's ODC brand is repeated over and over again on different surfaces. The one feature of the restaurant that prevails throughout is the use of white.

Designer: DENIS KOSUTIC
www.orlandodicastello.at
Location: VIENNA, AUSTRIA
Opening date: JUNE 2009
Photos: © LEA TITZ

THROUGH THE USE OF INVERTED OR DISTORTED PLANS AND PROPORTIONS, THE RESTAURANT TAKES ON A SURREAL APPEARANCE THAT IS FULL OF IRONIC ELEMENTS AND SURPRISES FOR DINERS.

The ODC logo is repeated on different surfaces, whether printed or applied to objects that have been made by hand.

ODC
O
DC
ODC
ODC
O

ODC

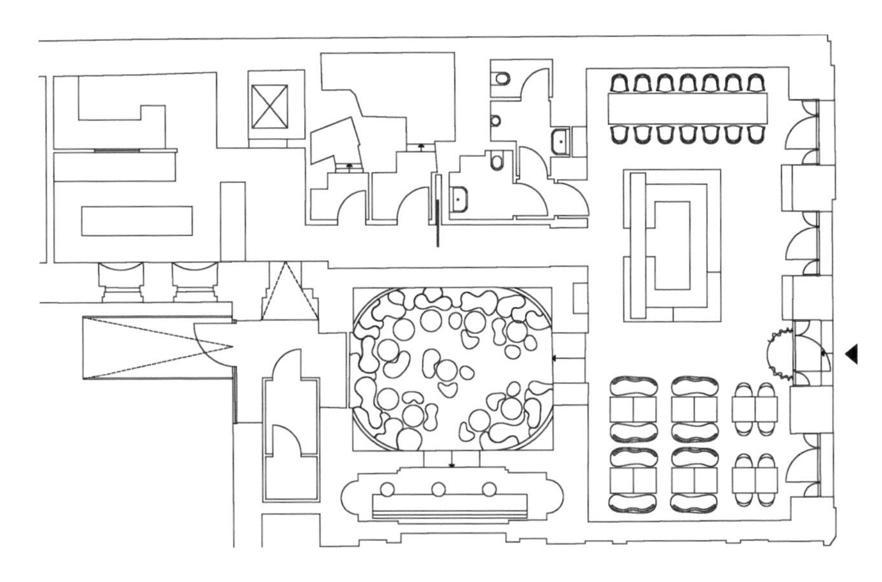

Floor plan

Dos Palillos

In addition to a formal invitation from Camper to design this restaurant located in their Berlin hotel, one of the things that encouraged the famous Bouroullec brothers, Ronan and Erwan, to participate in the project was the gastronomic proposal put forward by Albert Raurich, a former chef at El Bulli. The brothers, who were impressed by Raurich's fine cooking, designed a kitchen that not only occupies the center of the restaurant, but is also open enough for diners to be able to see how the food is prepared. And as there is only one long wooden table surrounding the workspace of the chefs, the chefs and diners frequently come face to face.

To focus attention on the cooking and away from distractions, the brothers designed the space to have a minimalistic feel. Its location, the ground floor of the Hotel Casa Camper in the Mitte district of Berlin, allows its huge windows to look onto the busy street. As diners enjoy the "show" the chefs put on in the kitchen, they too become actors, conversing and enjoying fine food in a "show" for passersby.

Designer: RONALD AND ERWAN BOUROULLEC
www.dospalillos.com
Location: BERLIN, GERMANY
Opening date: JANUARY 2010
Photos: © TAHON & BOUROULLEC

PATRONS CLOSELY WATCH THE WORK OF THE RESTAURANT'S TEN CHEFS AS IF THEY WERE ATTENDING AN ARTISTIC PERFORMANCE.

The Bouroullec brothers chose to forgo excess decorative elements to focus diners' attention on the kitchen.

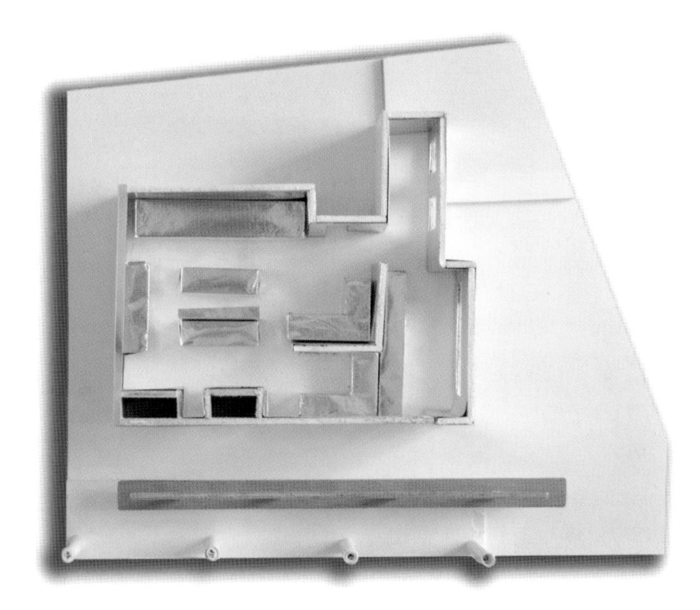

Model

Inamo

This establishment, specializing in pan-Asian food, occupies a surface area of about 3,300 square feet (306 square meters) and two floors: a restaurant upstairs and a bar below. Menus are projected onto each of the tables by means of individual interactive devices in the shape of a bud. In addition to ordering food and drinks, diners can use the devices to play games or search for information and local amenities.

Relying on the dark color of the ceiling and the flooring, the tables were specially designed to receive images from the projectors and serve as the focal point of the restaurant. The forward thinking that designers relied on to create their "kaleidoscope menu," also provided inspiration for creating origami panels on the walls. The panels contribute to the feeling of a nontraditional Asian atmosphere—one that is constantly changing like a kaleidoscope and like the menu.

Designer: BLACKSHEEP
www.inamo-restaurant.com
Location: LONDON, UK
Opening date: OCTOBER 2008
Photos: © FRANCESCA YORKE

THE AIM OF THE DESIGN FOR THIS VENUE WAS TO STRIKE A VISUAL BALANCE BETWEEN THE TECHNOLOGICAL ASPECTS OF THE RESTAURANT, ITS SENSUAL AMBIENCE, AND THE STRONG PERSONALITY AFFORDED TO IT BY ITS SOCIAL AREAS.

From the tables in the restaurant, which were specially designed with this venue in mind, it is possible for diners to see the chefs going about their work in real time.

Pomegranate Duck
Thai red curry
Pomegranate Duck
£16.40
Thai red curry
£3.00

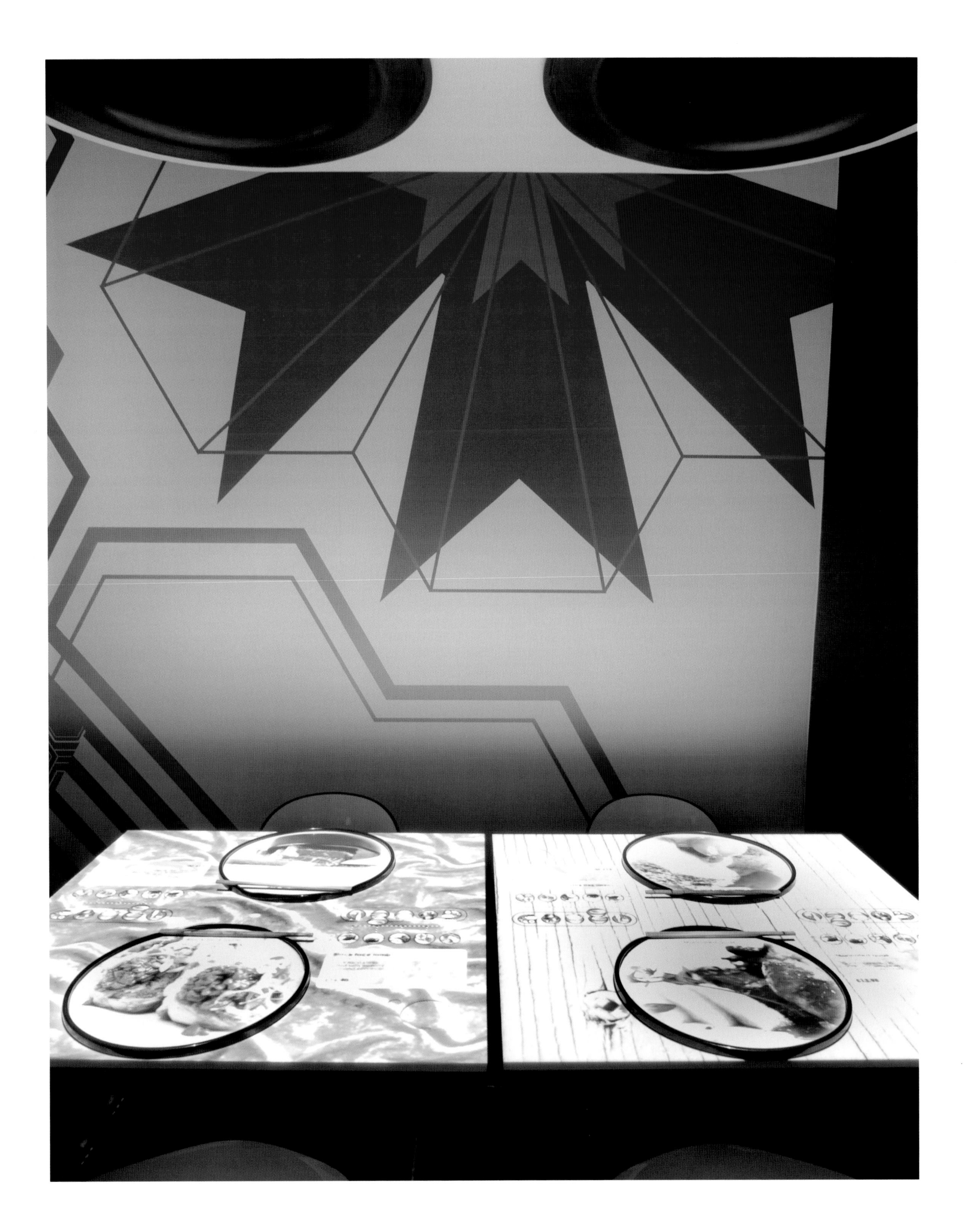

inamo

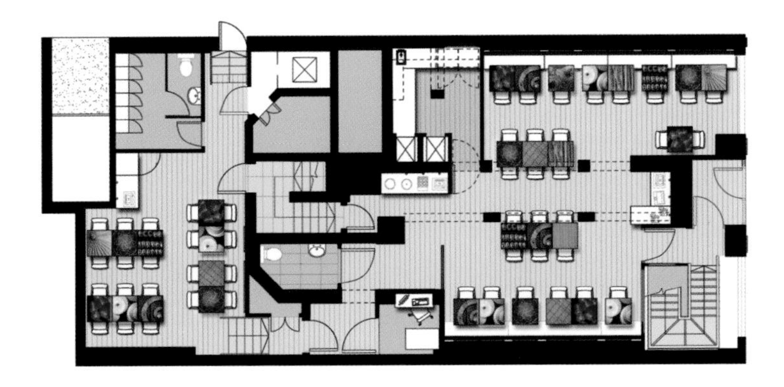

Floor plan

Restaurante Tartessos

Located at the very top of the new building housing Andalusia's Museum of Memory is a restaurant that offers panoramic views of the city and the Elvira mountain range. It is a long restaurant formed by a glass box, 131 feet (40 meters) long, 19 feet (six meters) wide, and nine feet (three meters) high, and it features a simple arrangement of an aisle down the center and tables along the sides. At one end of the restaurant, a glass area is partitioned off from the main room by a large bottle rack made of transparent polycarbonate.

The restaurant's floor is made of white marble from Macael. Its ceiling, along with its fitted lights, was painted in exactly the same gray as the exposed concrete. The simple forms and pure lines, as well as the open design of the area, generate a very peculiar feeling of space—something akin to the idea of literally floating on air.

Designer: ALBERTO CAMPO BAEZA.
www.restaurantetartessos.com
Location: GRANADA, SPAIN
Opening date: MAY 2009
Photos: © JAVIER CALLEJAS

THE VIEW OF THE CITY OF TARTESSOS IS MADE POSSIBLE BY THE RESTAURANT'S LOCATION ON THE TOP FLOOR OF THE SCREEN BUILDING, WHICH STANDS TALL ABOVE THE REST OF ANDALUSIA'S MUSEUM OF MEMORY.

The tables have stainless steel frames and black matte Formica tops. The chairs are designer Ludwig Mies van der Rohe's Brno model.

KIABI

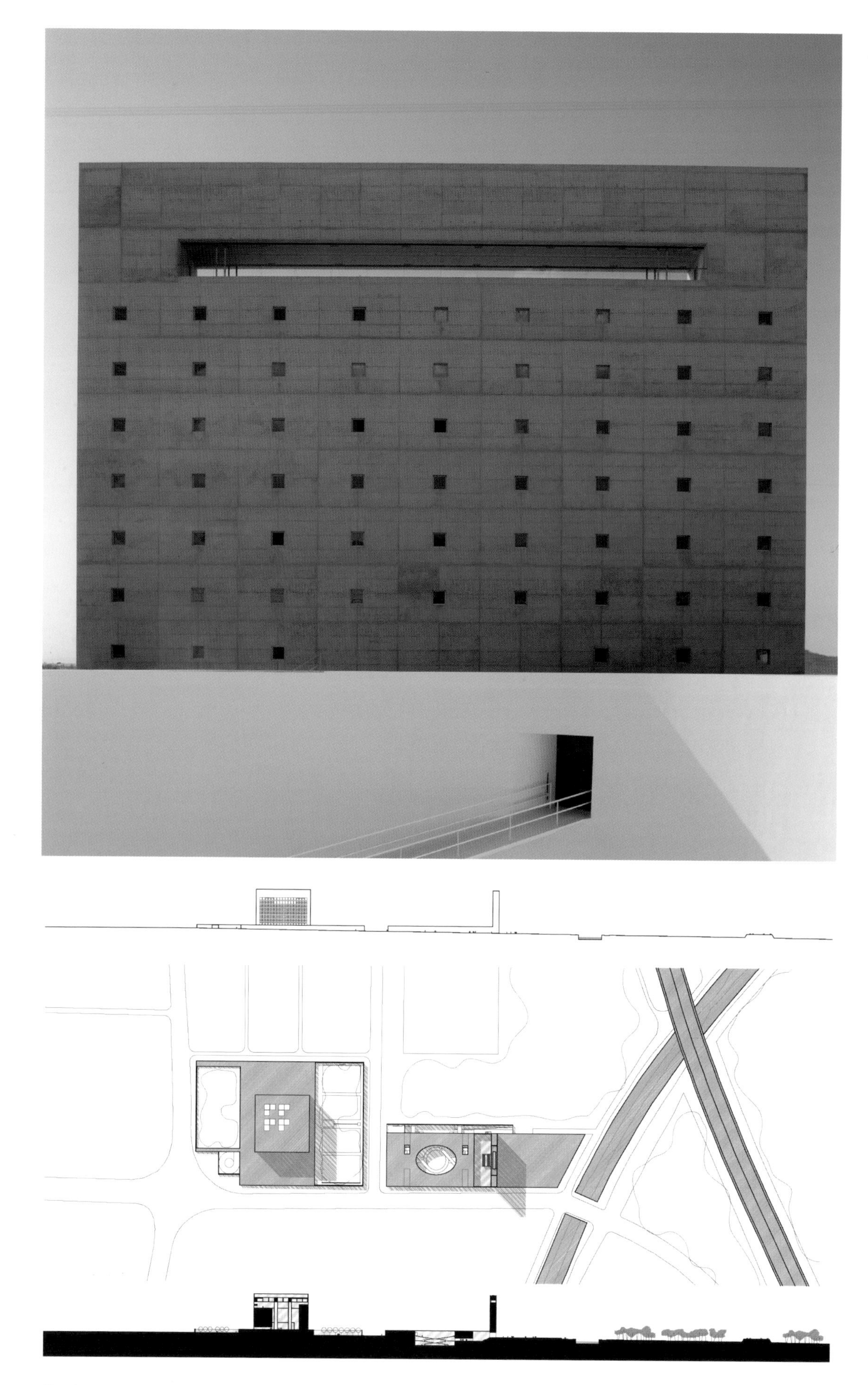

Site plan

GIACOMO
CHOOSE YOUR TASTE

Giacomo

For the design of this fast-food restaurant, the architects wanted to avoid falling into the trap of replicating the typical appearance of this type of venue, thereby hoping to prove that a quality design is possible in every kind of setting. For this reason, they resorted to an "international language" that mixes the light, fluid shapes common in Asian architecture with more contemporary elements. The result is a sensual ambience, with subtle lighting and surfaces that seem to float on air. The finishes and color schemes were selected to match the restaurant's corporate image and branding.

The original style of the ceiling remains exposed as an emotive component reflecting the history of the building. Despite the apparent simplicity of the design, a great deal of attention was paid to the technological and functional aspects of the restaurant. These are essential to keep it modern and to ensure a proper flow of work behind the counter.

Designer: PLAJER & FRANZ STUDIO
Location: BERLIN, GERMANY
Opening date: JUNE 2009
Photos: © KEN SCHLUCHTMANN/DIEPHOTODESIGNER.DE

WHEN DESIGNING THIS FAST-FOOD RESTAURANT, THE ARCHITECTS WANTED TO ENSURE A FEELING OF QUALITY AND AUTHENTICITY.

Various elements that respond to the corporate image of the restaurant chain were applied in a harmonious fashion and perfectly integrated into the overall design of the space.

GIACOMO
CHOOSE YOUR TASTE

GIACOMO
HEISSGETRÄNKE
KALTGETRÄNKE

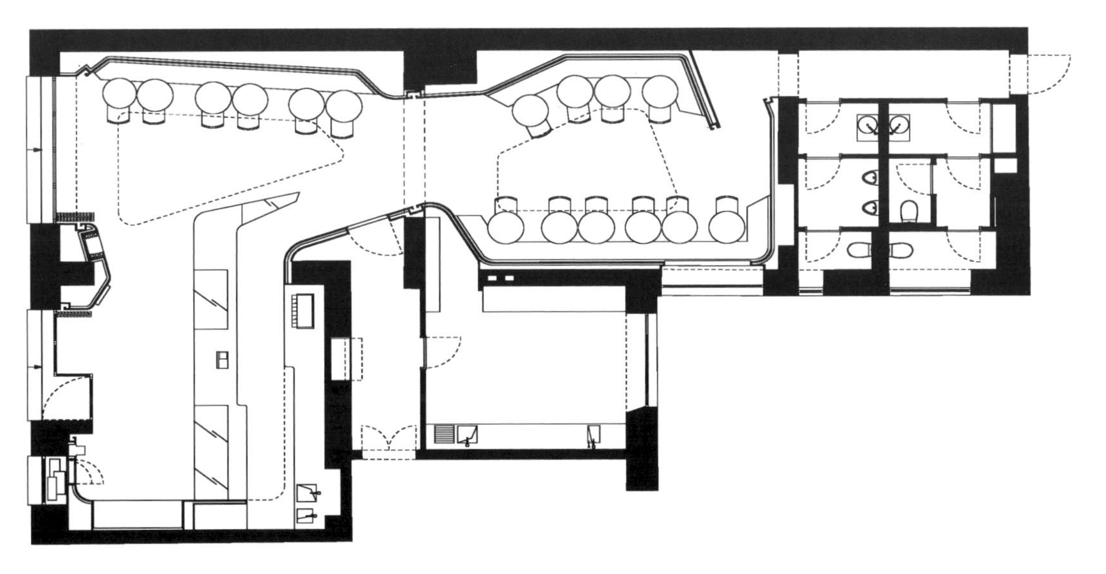

Floor plan

Big Fish

Located in an alley in Borne, one of Barcelona's fashionable districts, Big Fish is a "concept restaurant" founded by a family of fish merchants. The aim of its designers was to create an interior décor that is fresh and dynamic, incorporating both period furniture and accessories, along with other more modern supports for the restaurant's day-to-day needs.

One of the restaurant's main attractions is a huge light in a natural color. It is shaped like a waterfall and formed by dozens of discs made of seashells. The visual lightness of this piece contrasts with the old ship lanterns that surround the bar. The vintage-style dining room contains sofas—reminiscent of Chester models—with worn leather upholstery, but with their style intact. Alongside these sofas are chairs dating back to the middle of the century. The overall design is warm and inviting.

Designer: LÁZARO ROSA-VIOLÁN-CONTEMPORAIN STUDIO
www.bigfish.cat
Location: BARCELONA, SPAIN
Opening date: February 2009
Photos: © Margaret Stepien

VAPORES DE PINILLOS, IZQUIERDO Y Cª
PARA
ISLAS CANARIAS,
San Juan de Puerto Rico.
MAYAGUEZ,
PONCE, SANTIAGO DE CUBA,
Habana y New-Orleans
SALDRA DE CADIZ EL DIA 13 DE ABRIL
EL VAPOR
CATALINA
capitán D. Antonio Jaureguizar.
admite PASAJEROS de 1.ª,
2.ª y 3.ª clase y CARGA
para los referidos puertos.
Informarán sus armadores,
PINILLOS, IZQUIERDO Y Cª

FOUNDED BY A FAMILY OF FISH MERCHANTS, THE VISUAL IDENTITY OF THIS RESTAURANT IS FORMED BY REFERENCES TO THE OCEAN.

With its spectacular wooden bar and attractive rigging holding wine and liquor bottles, the bar evokes the charm of the taverns and inns of the nineteenth century.

Big FISH
Martini

ESTETICA

Café del Arco

A landmark center of cultural and leisure life in Murcia, Spain, the refurbishment of this café in the early 80's included extending its bar, positioning the bar better in relation to the terrace and transit areas, improving the kitchen facilities, and modernizing the overall look of the venue.

In order to create a continuous café-terrace space, a vertical surface was created that envelops the café without touching it, and curves inward to create different spatial areas. A partition composed of a succession of Iroko wood slats, slats on a hardwood made from Africa, on a galvanized and thermo-lacquered steel frame, provides rigidity to the structure. A line drawn on the paving that crosses the neighboring Plaza de la Teatro Romea flows into the interior of the building, reinforcing the idea of an "interiorized" outdoor area.

Designer: CLAVEL ARQUITECTOS
Location: MURCIA, SPAIN
Opening date: NOVEMBER 2009
Photos: © DAVID FRUTOS

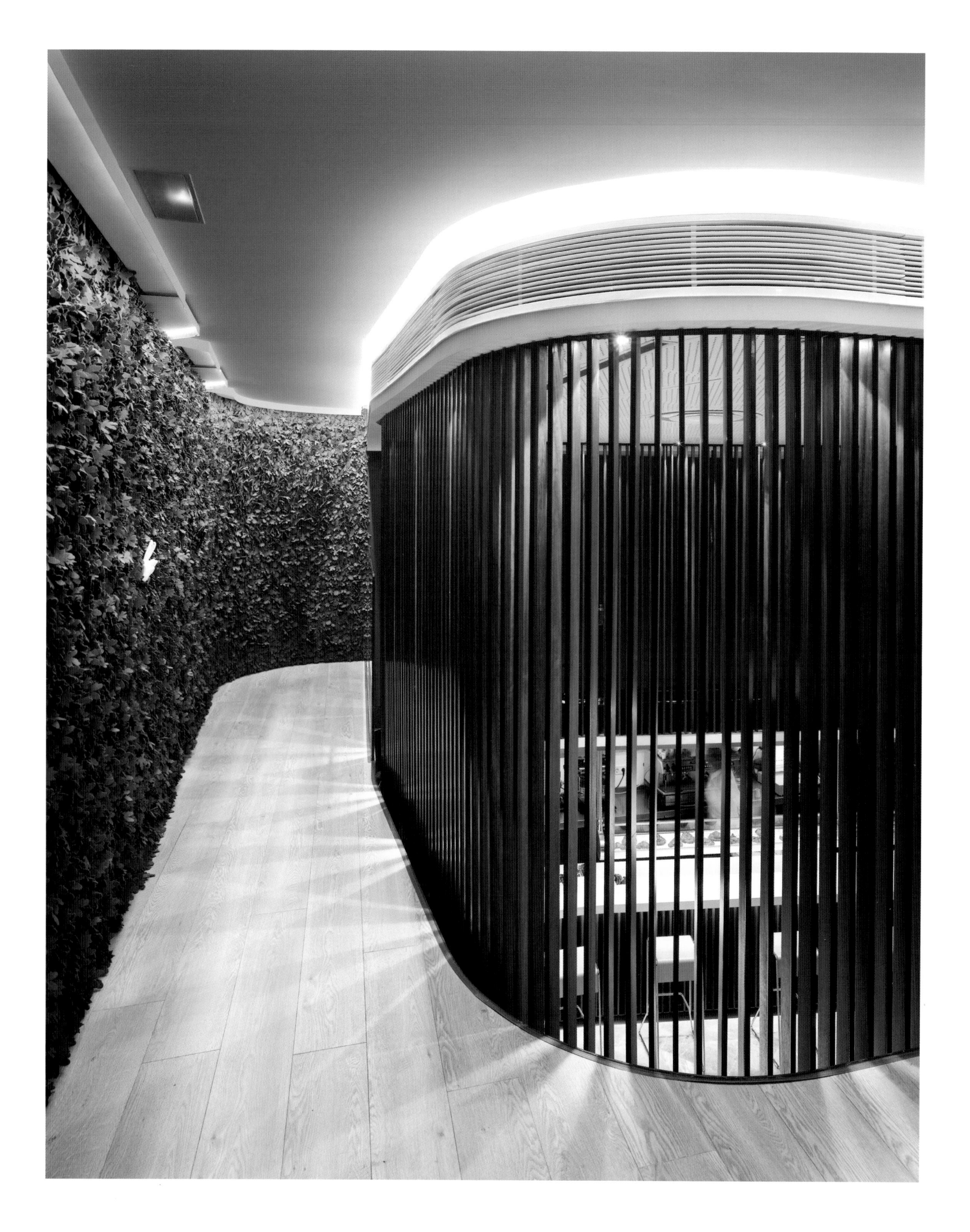

THE REFURBISHMENT OF THIS LANDMARK CAFÉ IN MURCIA, TRANSPOSES THE CONCEPTS OF EXTERIOR AND INTERIOR BY WAY OF A SERIES OF ARCHITECTURAL DESIGNS THAT BLUR TRADITIONAL BOUNDARIES.

The vertical design serves as a lattice between the mezzanine and the central space.

Intermon
Oxfam

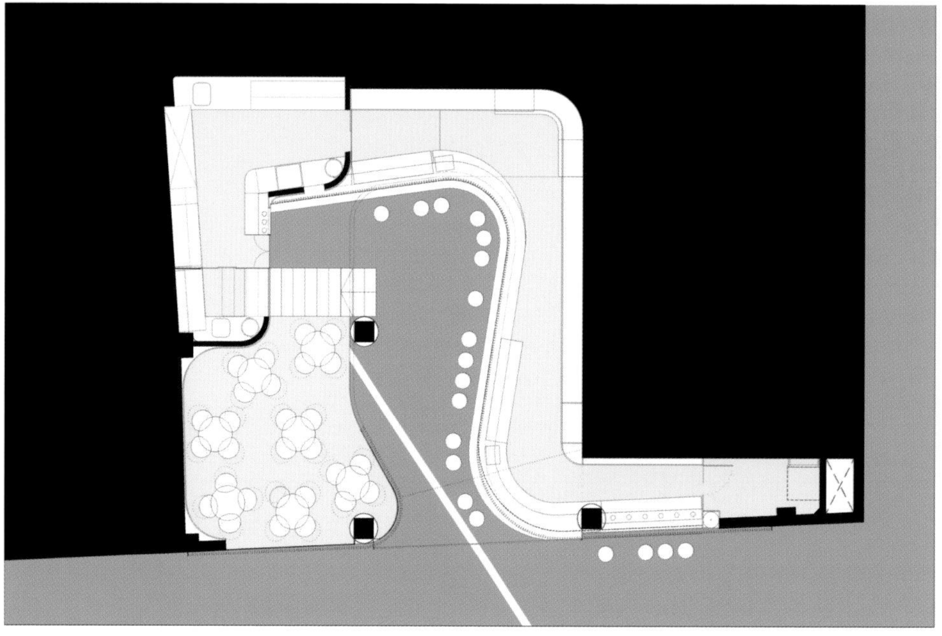

Floor plan

Mandi, Casa de Comidas

This restaurant is located in what used to be an impersonal office with several different floor levels in a building whose hidden facade meant it often went unnoticed. To transform the space, the architects focused on transparency, neutral plans, and a recurring play on light and reflections.

The interior design appears to be more than it actually is, playfully suggesting what is not there, and infusing the ambience with memories and sensations. The table tucked away in a library with family photographs, could be part of anyone's family dining room. Like the rest of the space, it is both personal and impersonal at the same time.

The restaurant's low ceilings appear to be higher than they actually are. This occurs because of a play on reflections and light, which is achieved by stretching shiny fabrics to achieve a "mirror effect," multiplying light, and thereby visually transforming the interior.

Designer: TOUZA Y ASOCIADOS
www.casamandi.es
Location: MADRID, SPAIN
Opening date: MARCH 2009
Photos: © LUCIO VÁZQUEZ/EL EQUIPO

EXQUISITE FURNISHINGS, AN ATTRACTIVE INTERPLAY OF LIGHT AND COLORS, AND A THOUGHTFUL USE OF GLASS AND REFLECTIONS, CREATE A TROMPE L'OEIL FOR THIS MADRID RESTAURANT.

A range of materials, such as velvet, silk, ebony, and glass, are boldly mixed together.

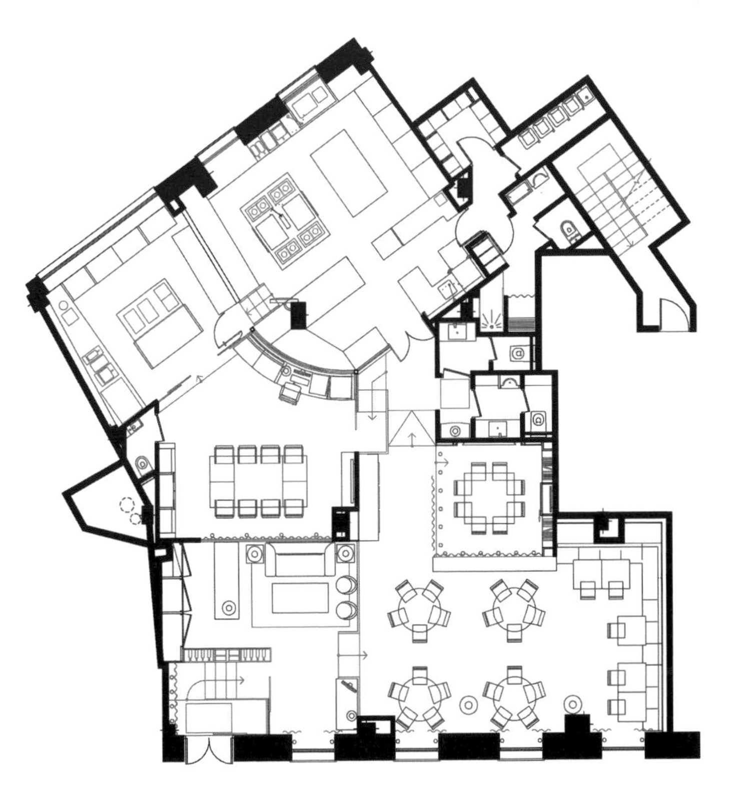

Floor plan

Café de la Reina

Café de la Reina brings a colorful and lighthearted note to the luxurious Reina Petronila hotel where it is located. A lobby connects the café with the hotel, and due to its versatile design, the establishment offers a range of services throughout the day. During the day, the café serves as a deli, awash with natural light. At night, its iridescent materials and watercolors transform the space into a vibrant bar.

The café's floor plan takes on an added dimension because of the large sinuous bar that runs the length of the premises and dictates the arrangement of its furnishings. The S-shaped benches and circular tables are a counterpoint to it, as is the deep blue color that contrasts with the bold green of the bar. A "lattice," made from pieces that resemble algae, camouflages the curtain wall of the facade and the more mundane views of the city, so that what remains clearly visible is visually enticing.

Designer: MONEO BROCK STUDIO
www.palafoxhoteles.com
Location: ZARAGOZA, SPAIN
Opening date: MARCH 2010
Photos: © BELÉN MONEO, LUIS ASÍN

SINUOUS LINES AND REFLECTIVE SURFACES GIVE A NEW DIMENSION TO THIS RESTAURANT, WHICH IS LOCATED IN A LUXURY HOTEL. ITS STYLE IS A SYNTHESIS OF RETRO AND MODERNITY CREATED THROUGH THE USE OF VIBRANT COLORS.

Gently undulating walls have reflective strips. Circular benches and tables help create a dynamic atmosphere.

ARAGONIA

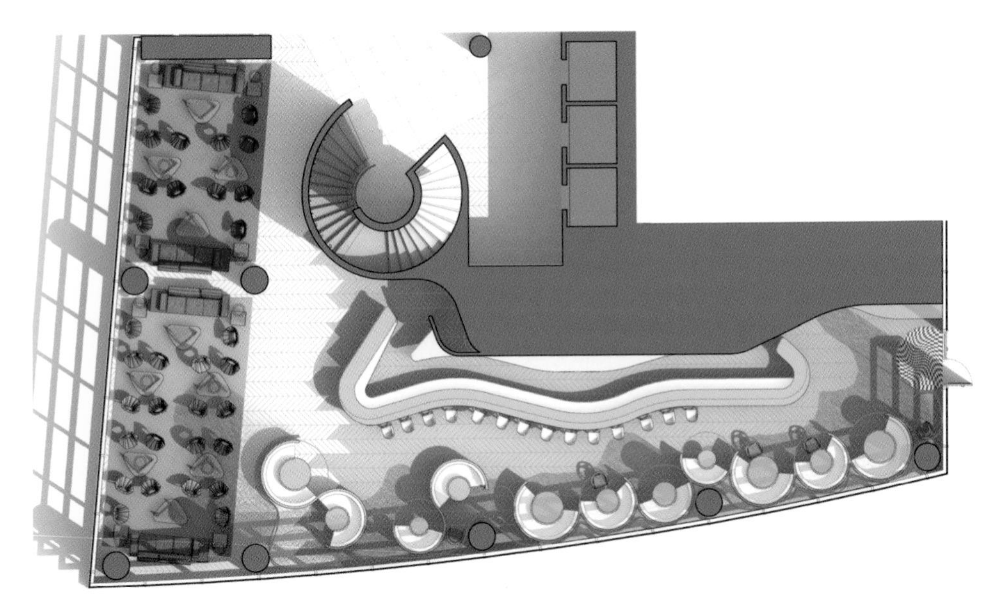

Floor plan

BECK'S
VIER
ABSOLUT
VODKA
JAMESON
ABSOLUT
VODKA

Profile Soho

This establishment has a New York vibe that creates a vibrant and attractive design. Its retro-style café and bar grants the use of shocking color combinations, like yellow and black. Bright chrome lamps highlight brick-shaped tiles on the walls. Upholstered seats stretch halfway up the wall. A central bar, illuminated with neon yellow and pink and surrounded by padded swivel chairs, is the focal point of the space. On one side of the restaurant, high tables and stools are enjoyed by small parties or those waiting on group reservations. A tiled walkway in the center of the aisle creates a visual dialogue with the lighting installation that lines the entire wall.

Designer: SHAUN CLARKSON
www.profilesoho.com
Location: LONDON, UK
Opening date: JULY 2009
Photos: © PROFILE SOHO

DINERS ENJOY THE RESTAURANT'S MENU, WHICH LIVES UP TO ITS REPUTATION FOR CLASSIC NEW YORK FARE—FROM DAILY BREAKFASTS TO MEATLOAF, CHEESEBURGERS, AND SPICY MEXICAN SAUSAGE.

A fifties vibe defines the tone for this restaurant and bar where the furniture and retro forms take on a contemporary and pop air thanks to a vibrant color scheme.

Motto

This bar has been carefully refurbished so as not to lose its connection with the history and heritage of its owners, who are famous in the city. Thus, the distribution of spaces and the furniture is comfortable, but not overtly sophisticated or modern.

The design of the restaurant was created through the use of different tones of color, clever detailing, and quality materials. More than four hundred plastic puppets hang from a vaulted ceiling. When the bar is busy, they appear to mix with the crowd in its vibrant, violet-tinged atmosphere.

For a clear and simple distribution, tables can be joined or separated as needed. Their purple fabric upholstery is covered in a plastic film, which reflects the light. The intense colors of the chairs and the tables, structured with mirrored tops, complete the composition.

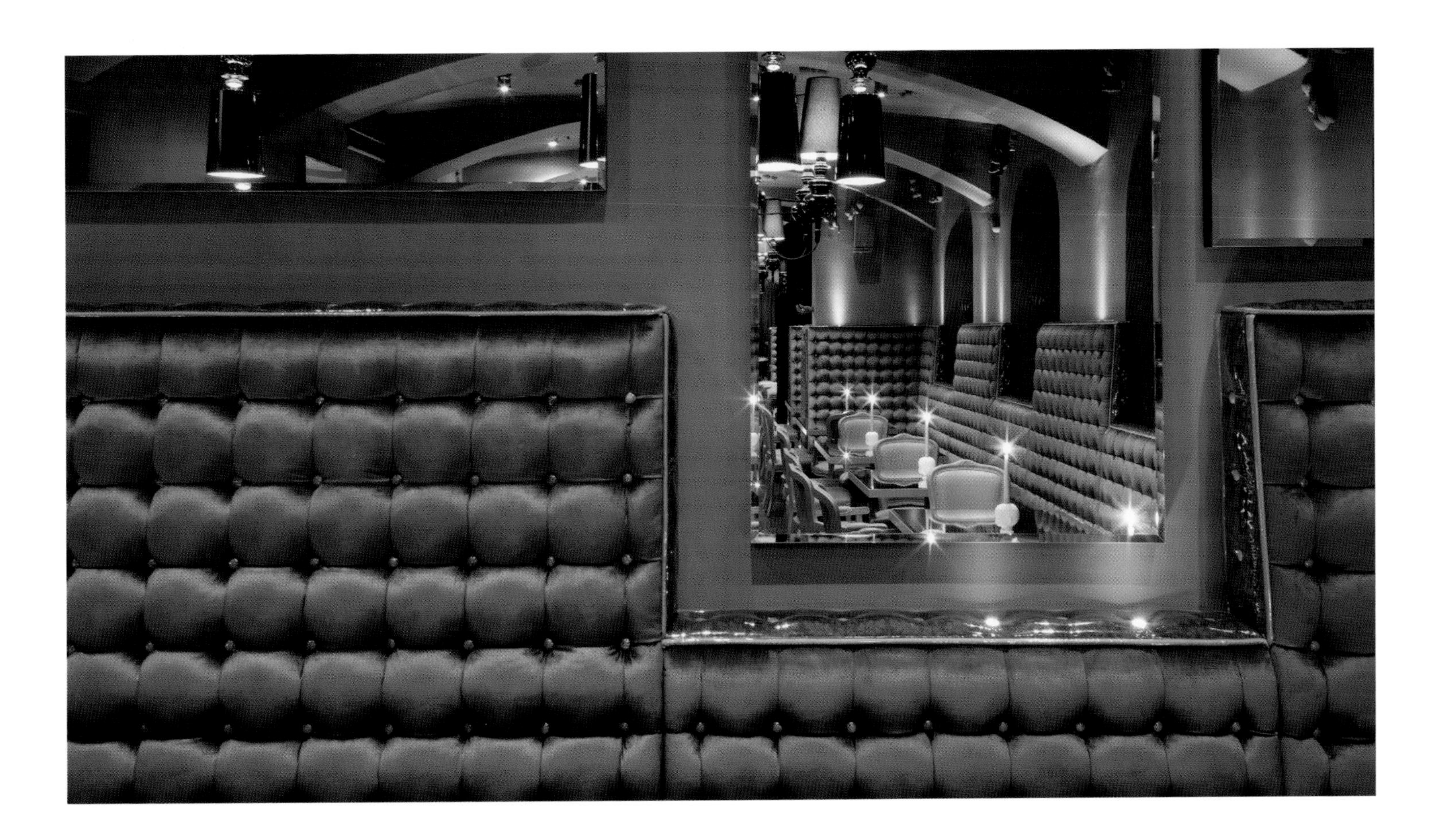

Designer: BEHF ARCHITECTS
www.motto.at/motto
Location: VIENNA, AUSTRIA
Opening date: AUGUST 2008
Photos: © PAUL OTT

EVEN AFTER THE REFURBISHMENT OF THIS TRENDY BAR, A STAPLE IN THE CITY OF VIENNA, COMFORT CONTINUES TO TAKE PRIORITY.

Turquoise, orange, and pink chairs contrast with the purple decor.

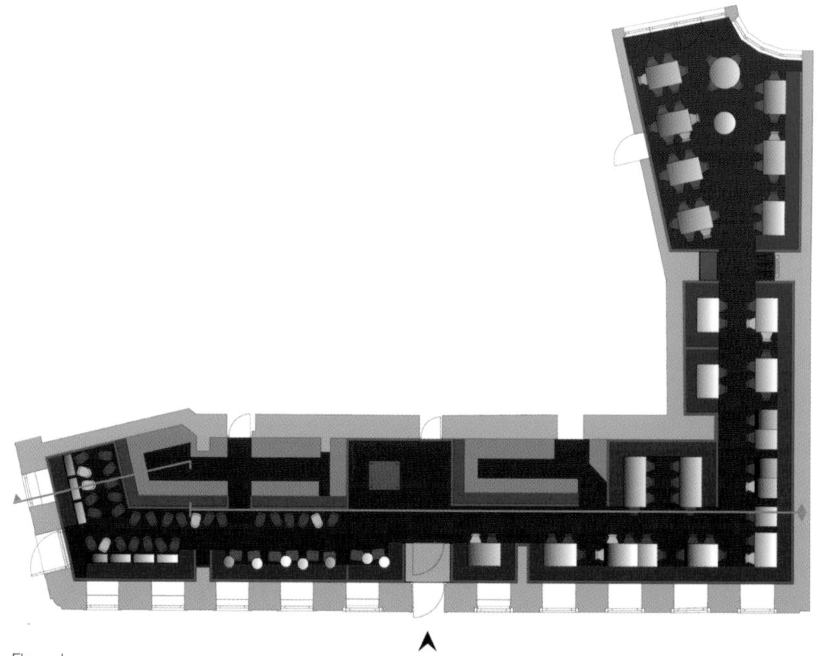

Floor plan

НАЧИНКИ МЯСНЫЕ
КУРА
ВЕТЧИНА
БЕФСТРОГАНОВ
СВИНИНА
НАЧИНКИ ОВОЩНЫЕ
ОВОЩИ ГРИЛЬ
ДОБАВКИ И СОУСЫ
ГРИБОЧКИ ЖАРЕНЫЕ 15р
СЫР СЛИВОЧНЫЙ 15р
ПОМИДОРНЫЙ ОСТРЫЙ СОУС 15р
ЧЕСНОЧНЫЙ СОУС 15р
СМЕТАНА 15р
МАЙОНЕЗ С ОГУРЧИКАМИ 15р
СОУС ГРИБНОЙ 15р
СОУС СЛИВОЧНЫЙ 15р
СОУС ХРЕНОВЫЙ 15р
ЗЕЛЕНЬ 15р
САЛАТЫ
СТОЛИЧНЫЙ 45р
РУССКИЙ С КУРИНОЙ ГРУДКОЙ 45р
ОВОЩНОЙ С СЫРОМ 45р
КОКТЕЙЛЬ 45р
ФРУКТЫ 45р
СУП
СУП ДНЯ 55р
НАПИТКИ
ЧАЙ В ЧАЙНИКЕ 45р
ЧАЙ ХОЛОДНЫЙ 45р
МОРС КЛЮКВЕННЫЙ 45р

Teaspoon

In order to create a contemporary space with a strong Russian identity—a goal far removed from the norm for this type of venue—the architects came up with a striking new design for this café, part of a chain that specializes in tea and pancakes. The most striking feature of the layout is a ceramic wall nearly twenty feet (six meters) high. For this, they chose the same orange as is used in the brand's corporate color, two stronger shades of it, as well as black and white to create contrast. Inspiration for the wall's design was drawn from the iconography of Russian folklore. Its enormity dominates the space.

The main dining room is a large, generous communal area with picnic-like tables. Some tables have benches. Others offer both individual or two-person seating units, to ensure that all the restaurant's customers, whether dining alone or in groups, feel comfortable.

Designer: SHH
www.teaspoon.ru
Location: ST. PETERSBURG, RUSSIA
Opening date: MAY 2008
Photos: © SHH

THE ARCHITECTS INTENDED TO CREATE A LARGE, CLEAR SPACE WITH PLENTY OF LIGHT. THEY ALSO SOUGHT TO DEVISE NEW WAYS OF USING THE ORANGE THAT IDENTIFIES THIS CHAIN OF RESTAURANTS.

The large variety of sizes, heights, and formats of the tables provides intimacy for small parties, as well as communal spaces for customers dining in groups.

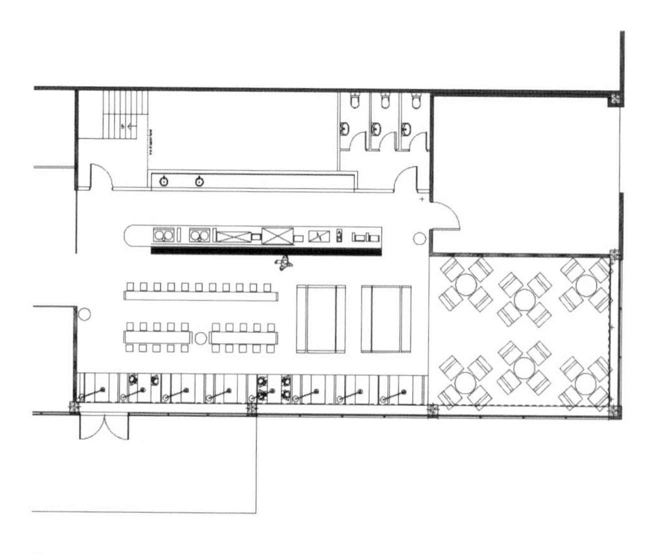

Floor plan

Access For

Open Kitchen Bar & Restaurant

This establishment is the training restaurant of the London City Hospitality Center in cooperation with the Hackney Community College, among other entities, and although open to the public, it is located on the college campus, in Shoreditch.

The homey, informal, and airy atmosphere is combined with handcrafted elements, stunning graphics, and clean finishes. The furniture, light fixtures, and art pieces were bought from local manufacturers.

The activity in the restaurant and kitchen can be watched through large windows. The back entrances now lead to the terrace. The main entrance is a green wall decked with potted plants, glass handrails, and a protective roof. Inside, the prevailing palette of vibrant colors highlights the furniture and lighting.

Designer: JESTICO + WHILES
www.openkitchen.biz
Location: LONDON, UK
Opening date: JUNE 2009
Photos: © AURELIEN THOMAS

THIS RESTAURANT, WHICH IS OPEN TO THE PUBLIC, TRAINS CULINARY STUDENTS IN THE CREATION OF INTERNATIONAL DISHES AND IN HOW TO SERVE COFFEE AND PASTRIES, A LIGHT LUNCH, AND A THREE-COURSE DINNER.

All graphics displayed on the windows and walls were designed by the architects.

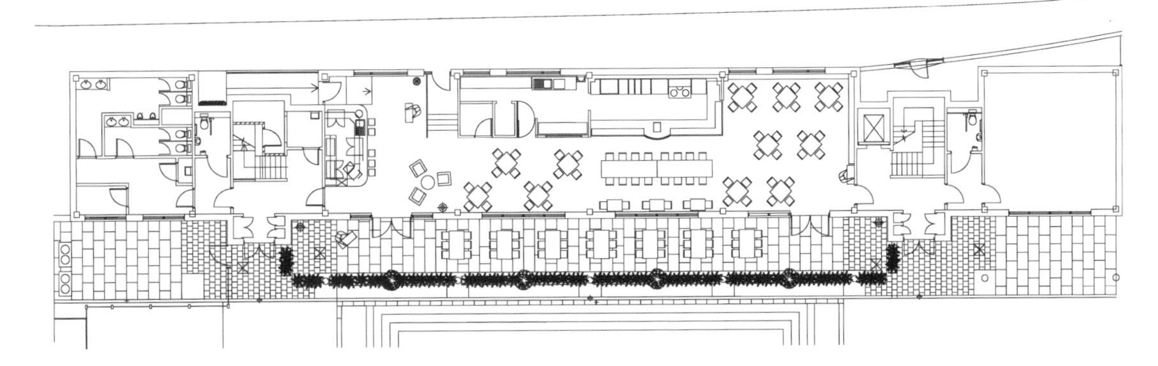

Floor plan

Corso Place Franz Liszt

This restaurant, part of the well-known Costes group of restaurants and hotels, is the second in a chain called Corso. In this location, the basic intent was to create a space using design elements without it looking like a restaurant design.

Thus the 1,507-square-foot (140 square meters) establishment is divided into two linked spaces, defined by an interior wall that seems to be perforated in a staggered manner. However, this effect is created with geometric-shaped mirrors that form an interesting two-tier effect.

The tables and the bar are made from Ductal concrete; a material that in addition to its interesting aesthetic value is both flexible and resistant. The lighting fixtures are the focus of attention for their size and quantity. To give the lamps a more dramatic and original look, metallic and reflective duct tape were used.

Designer: ROBERT STADLER (INTERIOR)
Location: PARIS, FRANCE
Opening date: SUMMER 2009
Photos: © MARC DOMAGE

THE INTERIOR OF THIS RESTAURANT IS HIGHLIGHTED BY THE PINK BAR MADE OF FLEXIBLE CEMENT AND THE HANGING LAMPS, WHICH HAVE GOLD-COLORED TAPE IN THE INTERIOR TO ENHANCE THE REFLECTION OF LIGHT.

The staggered mirrors are arranged to create a two-tier effect.

Divinatio

This restaurant, located in one of the piers of the port of Utrecht, occupies a building that it shares with the Visitors Center for the *Utrecht State-Yacht* (a boat rebuilt in the year 1746) and an information center. It is a four-story tower with a base of twenty-six by twenty-eight feet (nine by eight and a half meters) covered in dark gray brick. The winery is located below the water's surface.

The restaurant spaces are housed in boxes that protrude from the central tower, with varying depth, built in glass and steel. Thanks to these spectacular openings, diners have a privileged view of the port and can even clearly view Utrecht city center. The palette of the furniture and paneling has been limited to white, gray, and the wooden floor so as not to distract from the views.

Designer: ARCHITECTUURBUREAU SLUIJMER EN VAN LEEUWEN
www.divinatio.nl
Location: UTRECHT, THE NETHERLANDS
Opening date: JANUARY 2008
Photos: © CORNBREADWORKS

GLASS AND STEEL BOXES WERE CREATED ON THE FOUR SIDES OF THE CENTRAL TOWER TO MAKE THE RESTAURANT LARGER AND ARE HOME TO THE RESTAURANT'S TABLES.

The white tablecloths and the chairs reinforce the austere character of the interior in the marine ambience.

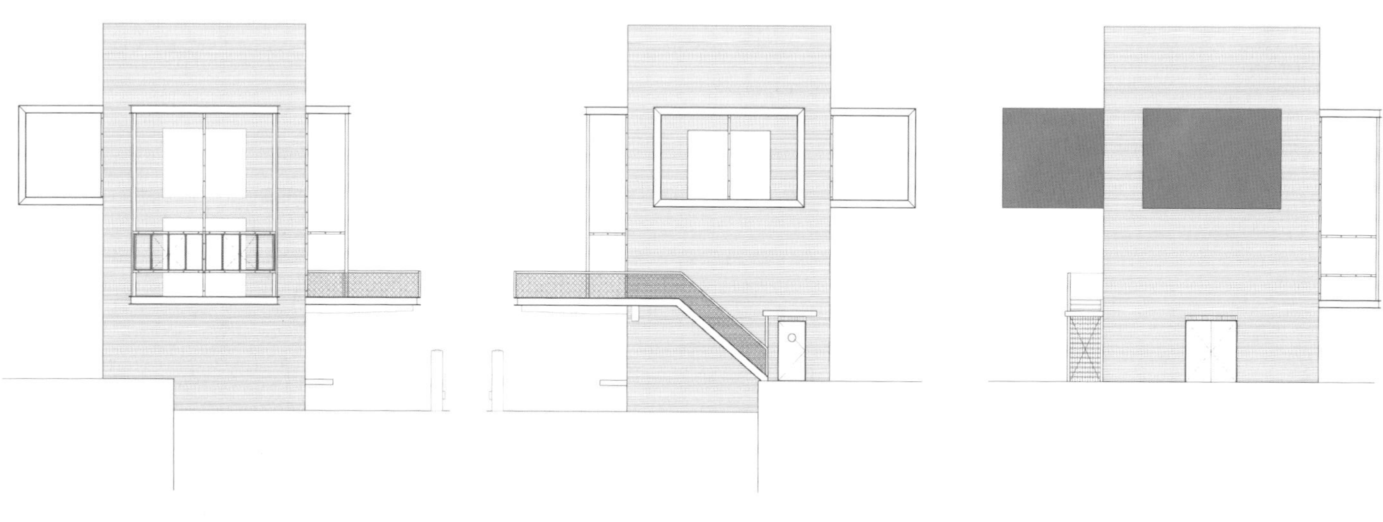

Elevations

Grand Café Usine

A former Philips tower where lamp bulbs were produced now houses a restaurant on the first floor of its iconic building. An old Philips poster with the caption "Les plus grandes usines du monde" was the inspiration for the restaurant. For the concept, this has been changed into "Usine le plus grand café du monde"—A grand cafe for everyone!

The entrance is a large space that allows guests to become familiar with the environment. This leads to the store and a second bar serving the terrace. The main bar, designed as a scaled-down version of the tower is located in the middle of the kitchen. The restaurant is divided into different areas, each with its own characteristics.

Through the large windows, an elevated wide step helps to lend the restaurant a more intimate character. As a result of a lack of space on the ground floor, the office hangs from the ceiling as if it were the deck for the factory supervisors.

Designer: BEARANDBUNNY
www.usine.nl
Location: EINDHOVEN, THE NETHERLANDS
Opening date: SUMMER 2009
Photos: © ARJEN SCHMITZ

THIS RESTAURANT, LOCATED IN AN OLD PHILIPS FACTORY, OFFERS A CONTEMPORARY INTERIOR DESIGN THAT CONFORMS TO THE EXISTING STRUCTURE AND CHARACTERISTICS OF THE BUILDING IN A NATURAL WAY.

The black-and-white tiled floor represents the original style of the factory, but the varying tile patterns in different areas of the restaurant gives an overall modern flair.

Weekgerechten
CUISINE
* Spinaziesalade
met feta € 7,90
* Koude komkommersoep
met tomaat € 4,30
Pizza Capricciosa
mozzarella,
artisjokken,
ham en olijven € 8,75
* Vegetarische € 14,20
groentencurry
met wilde rijst
* Gegrilde rode poon
met citroendille € 15,00
* Gebakken runder rib-eye
met kruidenboter
* Chocolade roomijs
met hollandse kersen

sits with a hairpin in her teeth

Blanc

A double-height atrium in shades of white is housed under an impressive glass ceiling in this lounge and restaurant of the Hotel Mandarin in Barcelona. The kitchen, run by Peter Zampaglione, the executive chef of the hotel, offers a menu based on seasonal ingredients with a nod to contemporary Asian cuisine and specialties from all over Spain.

The restaurant is divided into different spaces defined by how the furniture is put together. Crinoline outdoor fiber chairs designed by Urquiola, and plants hung at different levels lend the space an overall relaxed and leisurely feel.

The white perforated metal screens give a glimpse of the lobby and generate an interesting play of overlapped textures and effects of natural light that go all the way up to the ceiling. These figures visually communicate with the rug, which was specially handmade for the space.

Designer: PATRICIA URQUIOLA
www.mandarinoriental.com/barcelona
Location: BARCELONA, SPAIN
Opening date: NOVEMBER 2009
Photos: © JORDI MIRALLES

WITH A MENU THAT INCLUDES MEDITERRANEAN AND ASIAN SPECIALTIES, THE BLANC RESTAURANT AND LOUNGE ENJOYS LOTS OF NATURAL LIGHT FILTERING THROUGH ITS WHITE PERFORATED METAL SCREENS.

Almost all the furniture has been designed or adapted for this space.

Restaurante Trobador

In the chain's first premises in Madrid, the architects have taken characteristic elements from the company and presented them in a different light, such as the images, decorative lamps, and diamonds. Fine materials such as light wood, iron plates, and black glasses are predominant. Ambient light originates from cloth-covered light boxes.

The restaurant is spread over two levels that combine customer zones and areas for private use. Downstairs, the focus is the brasserie bar, consisting of transparent and opaque glass, iron, and wood.

In the basement, a set of two red tables takes the center stage and is backed by a rhythmic sequence of black diamond shelves. Here there is also a private space, which is separated by a chain curtain with white and red printed graphics. The restrooms extend the use of materials with a semi-open washbasin.

Designer: GCA ARQUITECTOS ASOCIADOS
www.restaurantetrobador.com
Location: MADRID, SPAIN
Opening date: JANUARY 2009
Photos: © JORDI MIRALLES

THE RESTAURANT IS CHARACTERIZED BY HAVING A SINGLE INTERIOR, WHERE THE VIVID THEATRICAL NATURE OF THE PICTURES ON THE WALLS AND LAMPS IS THE LEITMOTIF OF THE PROJECT.

The designer tables combine wood and iron, and the chairs are custom printed with subtle images of icons in their upholstery.

Vittoria Bar & Club

The Vittoria Bar & Club is located in a white concrete building that stands out due to its arc-shaped roof. A vast, black iron sliding door provides access to the bar, made luminous thanks to the light-colored polished concrete on all surfaces. The spiral staircase, also made of iron, leads to the tasting area and cellar on the lower level and to the machinery installations on the upper level.

The bar can be accessed through a corridor formed by two capacious black-stained oak wooden boxes. The right box houses a display case with select products, and the left box holds the restrooms.

The bar is made of a large slab of granite stone and the bottles are stored in glass-enclosed square openings that look like light boxes. Opposite, an oak bench runs the length of the bar from which platforms emerge that transform into sofas.

Designer: FRANCESC RIFÉ
Location: VITORIA-GASTEIZ, SPAIN
Opening date: OCTOBER 2008
Photos: © EUGENI PONS

THE ROOF HAS BEEN DESIGNED TO MAINTAIN THE ORIGINAL STRUCTURE. THE SPOTLIGHTS, SPEAKERS, AND AIR-CONDITIONING OUTLETS ARE RANDOMLY DISTRIBUTED ON THE CEILING, TAKING ADVANTAGE OF THE EXISTING ROOF SKYLIGHTS.

The bar is lit up by an impressive lamp designed by the architect. It sits below an iron structure painted the same color as the ceiling and walls.

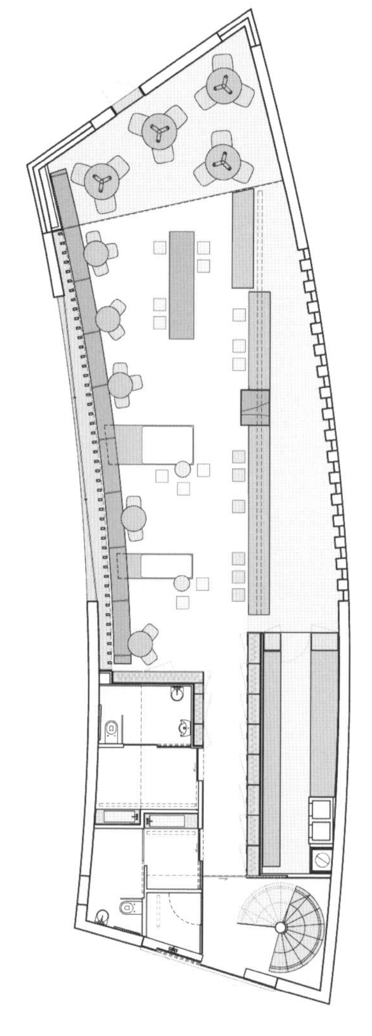

Floor plan

THEHOUSE | CAFÉ

The House Café Kanyon

The latest branch of The House Café chain at Istanbul's Kanyon mall is a succesful integration with the mall's original architecture. A site-built structure made of steel and glass that functions as a transparent box to house the café is designed to fit in with the architecture of the mall. The café's framework is situated on a walnut platform to add warmth to its interior.

There are two steps highlighted by a line of yellow light at the entrance of the restaurant. Wood is used for the back wall and bar shelves opposite the entrance. The furniture has been designed by the same architectural firm that designed the venue. The individual tables have marble tops, while the medium and large tables are entirely made of wood. The café's transparency visually widens its boundaries and connects it with the mall, however, its main function is to let natural light in.

Designer: AUTOBAN
www.thehousecafe.com.tr
Location: ISTANBUL, TURKEY
Opening date: APRIL 2009
Photos: © ALI BEKMAN

ALTHOUGH AN EXTENSION OF THE ARCHITECTURE OF THE MALL, THE STRUCTURE BEARS ITS OWN STRONG DESIGN IDENTITY WHILE BLENDING IN WITH ITS SURROUNDINGS.

A large iron pedestal contains a huge plant to fit in with the green of the building's surroundings.

EXIT

Directory of Architects

Aidlin Darling Design
San Francisco, CA, USA
www.aidlindarlingdesign.com

Alberto Campo Baeza
Madrid, Spain
www.campobaeza.com

Andre Kikoski Architect
New York, NY, USA
www.akarch.com

Architectuurbureau Sluijmer
en van Leeuwen
Utrecht, The Netherlands
www.architectuurbureau.nl

Arkhefield
Brisbane, Australia
www.arkhefield.com.au

Autoban
Istanbul, Turkey
www.autoban212.com

AvroKO
New York, NY, USA
www.avroko.com

Bearandbunny
Amsterdam, The Netherlands
www.bearandbunny.com

BEHF Architects
Vienna, Austria
www.behf.at

Blacksheep
London, United Kingdom
www.blacksheep.uk.com

Carlo Ratti Associati
Turin, Italy
www.carloratti.com

Clavel Arquitectos
Murcia, Spain
http://clavel-arquitectos.com

Concrete Architectural Associates
Amsterdam, The Netherlands
www.concreteamsterdam.nl

D-ash Design
Long Island City, NY, USA
www.davidashendesign.com

Denis Košutić
Vienna, Austria
www.deniskosutic.com

Design Spirits
Tokyo, Japan
www.design-spirits.com

Francesc Rifé
Barcelona, Spain
www.rife-design.com

GCA Arquitectos Asociados
Barcelona, Spain
www.gcaarq.com

Gow Hastings Architects
Toronto, Canada
Ontario, Canada
www.gowhastings.com

Graft
Los Angeles, CA, USA
Berlin, Germany
Beijing, China
www.graftlab.com

James & Mau
Madrid, Spain
Curacaví, Chile
Bogotá, Colombia
www.jamesandmau.com

Jestico + Whiles
London, United Kingdom
www.jesticowhiles.com

Kearns Mancini Architects
Toronto, Canada
Ontario, Canada
www.kmai.com

Lázaro Rosa-Violán Contemporain Studio
Barcelona, Spain
www.lazarorosaviolan.com

Manuel Villa
Bogotá, Colombia
www.manuelvillaarq.com

Matali Crasset
Paris, France
www.matalicrasset.com

Marc Newson
London, United Kingdom
www.marc-newson.com

Moneo Brock Studio
Madrid, Spain
www.moneobrock.com

Nema Workshop
New York, NY, USA
www.nemaworkshop.com

Nikken Sekkei
Tokyo, Japan
www.nikken.co.jp

Patricia Urquiola
Milan, Italy
www.patriciaurquiola.com

Pierluigi Piu
Cagliari, Italy
www.pierluigipiu.it

Philippe Starck
Paris, France
www.starck.com

Plajer & Franz Studio
Berlin, Germany
www.plajer-franz.de

Project Orange
London, United Kingdom
www.projectorange.com

Roman and Williams Building and Interiors
New York, NY, USA
www.romanandwilliams.com

Ronan & Erwan Bouroullec
Paris, France
www.bouroullec.com

Sandra Tarruella Interioristas
Barcelona, Spain
www.sandratarruella.com

Sebastian Mariscal Studio
San Diego, CA, USA
www.sebastianmariscal.com

Serie Architects
London, United Kingdom
Mumbai, India
www.serie.co.uk

Shaun Clarkson
London, United Kingdom
www.shaunclarksonid.com

SHH
London, United Kingdom
www.shh.co.uk

Slick+design
Chicago, IL, USA
Tampa, FL, USA
www.slickdesign.com

Stanley Saitowitz/Natoma Architects
San Francisco, CA, USA
www.saitowitz.com

Studio MK27
São Paulo, Brazil
www.marciokogan.com.br

Studio Robert Stadler
Paris, France
www.robertstadler.net

Takeshi Hosaka Architects
Kanagawa, Japan
www.hosakatakeshi.com

Touzay Asociados
Madrid, Spain
www.touza.com

Walter Barda Design
Sydney, Australia
www.walterbardadesign.com

Directory of Bars & Restaurants

BAR ASTRID Y GASTÓN
Carrera 7, 67-64
Bogotá, Colombia
P: +571 211 1400
www.astridygaston.com

BEIJING NOODLE No. 9
Caesars Palace Las Vegas
3570 Las Vegas Blvd. South
Las Vegas, NV 89109
USA
P: +1 877 346-4642
www.caesarspalace.com

BIG FISH
Carrer Comercial 9
08003 Barcelona, Spain
P: +34 93 268 17 28
www.bigfish.cat

BLANC
Passeig de Gràcia 38-40
08007 Barcelona, Spain
P: +34 93 151 87 83
www.mandarinoriental.com/
barcelona/dining/blanc

BOMMIE RESTAURANT
Hamilton Island, Great Barrier Reef, Australia
P: +61 7 4948 9433
www.hamiltonislandyachtclub.com.au

BRAND STEAKHOUSE
Monte Carlo Hotel
3770 Las Vegas Blvd. South
Las Vegas, NV 89109
USA
P: +1 702 730-6700
www.lightgroup.com/dining/
brand-steakhouse-las-vegas

CAFÉ DE LA REINA
Hotel Reina Petronila – Palafox Hoteles
Marqués de Casa Jiménez s/n.
50004 Zaragoza, Spain
P: +34 976 23 77 00
www.palafoxhoteles.com

CAFÉ DEL ARCO
Calle Arco de Santo Domingo 1
30001 Murcia, Spain
P: +34 968 21 97 67

CAFÉ TRUSSARDI
Piazza della Scala, 5
20121 Milan, Italy
+39 02 80688295
www.trussardi.com

CASA LEVER
390 Park Ave
New York, NY 10022
USA
P: +1 212 888-2700
www.casalever.com

CHARRO RESTAURANTE
729 N. Milwaukee St.
Milwaukee, WI 53202
USA
P: +1 414 431-5557
www.charrorestaurante.com

CORSO PLACE FRANZ LISZT
2, Place Franz Liszt
Paris 765010, France
P: +33 1 42 47 01 23

DE BIJENKORF KITCHEN
Dam 1
1012 JS Amsterdam, The Netherlands
P: +31 0900 0919
www.debijenkorf.nl

DELICATESSEN
54 Prince St.
New York, NY 10012
USA
P: +1 212 226-0211
www.delicatessennyc.com

DIVINATIO
Veilinghavenkade 14
3521 AK Utrecht, The Netherlands
P: +31 30 294 12 26
www.divinatio.nl

DOS PALILLOS
Weinmeisterstraße 1
10178 Berlin, Germany
P: +49 30 20003413
www.dospalillos.com

ESTADO PURO
Plaza Cánovas del Castillo, 4
28014 Madrid, Spain
P: +34 91 330 24 00
www.tapasenestadopuro.com

FORNERIA SAN PAOLO
Rua Amauri, 319
Itaim Bibi – Zona Sul
São Paulo, Brazil
P: +55 11 3078 0099
www.restauranteforneria.com.br

GIACOMO
Bleibtreustraße 32
10707 Berlin Germany
P: +49 030 8871 1688
www.giacomo.ag

GRAND CAFÉ USINE
Lichttoren 6
5611 BJ Eindhoven, The Netherlands
P: +31 40 2171890
www.usine.nl

HOTO FUDO
Fuji Kawaguchiko, Minamituru-gun
Yamanashi, Japan
P: +81 555 720 788
www.houtou-fudou.jp

INAMO
134-136 Wardour St.
Soho, London, W1F 8ZP
UK
P: +44 20 7851 7051
www.inamo-restaurant.com

I-T.ALIA
Shop #309 & 310, DLS Promenada
Nelson Mandela Marg,
Vasant Kunj, Delhi 110072, India
P: +91 011 43111777

LA XINA
Pintor Fortuny, 1
08001 Barcelona, Spain
P: +34 93 342 96 28
www.grupotragaluz.com

MANDI, CASA DE COMIDAS
Calle Almagro 20,
28010, Madrid, Spain
P: +34 91 310 45 20
www.casamandi.es

MERCAT A LA PLANXA
638 South Michigan Ave.
Chicago, IL 60605
USA
P: +1 312 765-0524
www.mercatchicago.com

MOTTO
Schönbrunnerstrasse 30
1050 Vienna, Austria
P: +43 1 587 06 72
www.motto.at/motto

NAUTILUS PROJECT
Ion Orchard
2 Orchard Turn, # 04-09
Singapore, 238801 Singapore
P: +65 6509 1033
www.thenautilusproject.com

OPEN KITCHEN BAR & RESTAURANT
40 Hoxton St.
London N1 6LR
UK
+ 44 20 7613 9590
www.openkitchen.biz

ORLANDO DI CASTELLO RESTAURANT
Freyung 1
1010 Vienna, Austria
P: +43 1 533 76 29
www.orlandodicastello.at

PARK AVENUE
100 East 63rd St.
New York, NY 10021
USA
P: + 212 644-1900
www.parkavenyc.com

LES PASTILLES
Avenue Eugène Donadeï
06703 Nice, France
P: +33 4 9331 1035
www.cap3000.com

PEARLS & CAVIAR
Qaryat Al Beri
Between the Bridges
Abu Dhabi, United Arabs Emirates
P: +971 2 509 8777
www.pearlsandcaviar.com

PIO PIO RESTAURANT
604 10th Ave.
New York, NY 10036
USA
P: +1 212 459-2929
www.piopionyc.com

PROFILE SOHO
84-86 Wardour Street
London W1F 0TQ
UK
P: +44 20 7734 3444
www.profilesoho.com

RESTAURANTE TARTESSOS
Avda. de las Ciencias 2
Centro Cultural Memoria de Andalucía
18006, Granada, Spain
P: +34 958 123 257
www.restaurantetartessos.com

RESTAURANTE TROBADOR
Paseo de Recoletos 14
28001, Madrid, Spain
P: +34 91 576 34 29
www.restaurantetrobador.com

RISTORANTE OLIVOMARE
10 Lower Belgrave St.
London SW1W 0LJ
UK
P: +44 020 7730 9022
www.olivorestaurants.com

TEASPOON
O'Key Shopping Mall
Balkanskaya St.,
St. Petersburg, Russia
P: +7 812 363 27 92
www.teaspoon.ru

THE BAZAAR BY JOSÉ ANDRÉS
465 South La Cienega Blvd.
Los Angeles, CA 90048
USA
P: +1 310 247-0400
www.thebazaar.com

THE CHEFS' HOUSE RESTAURANT
215 King Street East
Toronto, Ontario, M5A 1J9
Canada
P: +1 416 415-2260
www.thechefshouse.com

THE HOUSE CAFÉ KANYON
Kanyon Alışveriş Merkezi 185
Levent, Istanbul
Turkey
P: +90 212 353 5375
www.thehousecafe.com.tr

THE STANDARD GRILL
AND THE STANDARD CLUB
848 Washington St.
New York, NY 10014
USA
P: +1 212 645-4100
www.thestandardgrill.com

THE TOTE
Keshavarao Khadye Marg, Tulsiwadi
Mumbai, Maharashtra 400034, India
P: +91 22 6157 7777

THE WRIGHT
Guggenheim Museum
1071 Fifth Ave.
New York, NY 10128
USA
P: +1 212 427-5690
www.guggenheim.org/new-
york/visit-us/restaurants

TOAST
5800 Nave Dr.
Novato, CA 94949
USA
P: +1 415 382-1144
www.toastnovato.com

URBAN FARMER
525 SW Morrison St.
Portland, OR 97204
USA
P: +1 503 222-4900
www.urbanfarmerrestaurant.com

URBANE
179 Mary St.
Brisbane QLD 4000, Australia
P: +61 7 3229 2271
www.urbanerestaurant.com

U: PONTE VECCHIO
541-0042 Yodoyabashiodona 2F 4-1-1
Imabashi Chuo-ku, Osaka, Japan
P: +81 6 6205-0500
www.ponte-vecchio.co.jp

VITTORIA BAR & CLUB
Tanis Aguirrebengoa, 2
01007 Vitoria, Spain
P: +34 945 235 591

WHISKY MIST AT ZETA
35 Hertford St.
Mayfair, London W1J 7SD
UK
P: +44 20 7208 4067
www.whiskymist.com